# How to Get Your Book Reviewed

Sell More Books with Reviews, Testimonials and Endorsements

Dana Lynn Smith

Copyright © 2011 Dana Lynn Smith
All rights reserved.

Published by The Savvy Book Marketer
an imprint of Texana Publishing Consultants, LLC

www.TheSavvyBookMarketer.com

ISBN: 0-9823804-0-2
ISBN-13: 978-0-9823804-0-6

This is an informational guide and is not intended as a substitute for legal or other professional services. Readers are urged to consult a variety of sources and educate themselves about the business of publishing and marketing. While every effort has been made to make this guide accurate, it may contain typographical and content errors.

The information expressed herein is the opinion of the author, and is not intended to reflect upon any particular person or company. The author and publisher shall have no responsibility or liability with respect to any loss or damage caused, or alleged to be caused, by the information or application of the information contained in this guide.

# Praise for *How to Get Your Book Reviewed*

"A no-nonsense, richly-detailed examination of what you should and shouldn't be doing to ensure your book wends its way to the best hands available to promote your project, *How to Get Your Book Reviewed* is a quick and incredibly informative read."

— Glenn Dallas, San Francisco/Sacramento Book Reviews

"The thought of getting book reviews has been an intimidating area for me. I kept thinking, how am I going to do this as a new independent author? This book showed me every aspect of obtaining reviews from so many different sources. It covers every detail as well as offering invaluable links to many of the resources needed."

— Mal Duane, author of *Alpha Chick, Five Steps for Moving from Pain to Power*

"This is one the most comprehensive resources I've seen on how to generate book reviews. It's packed with "here's how to do it" information that authors need. I highly recommend it!"

— Sandra Beckwith, editor & publisher, *Build Book Buzz* free e-newsletter

"The potential that reviews have to boost an author from obscurity into the stratosphere are mind-boggling. *How to Get Your Book Reviewed* is the definitive guide for any writer who wants to get their book noticed. I highly recommend this book!"

— Fiona Ingram, author of *The Secret of the Sacred Scarab*

"Filled with rich content to make the effort easy, this ebook is the premier go-to manual for authors seeking book reviews."

— **Yvonne Perry, owner of Writers in the Sky Creative Writing Services**

"Here's a book designed to help you navigate the enormous world of book reviews as a marketing tool for your publishing project. I recommend *How to Get Your Book Reviewed* for all authors."

— **Patricia Fry, author of *Promote Your Book* and Executive Director of Small Publishers, Artists and Writers Network**

"After releasing (and seeking reviews for) six books, I thought I knew it all, but this book gave me some wonderful new tips and strategies. Recommended for novice and experienced authors alike!"

— **Heather Wardell, author of *Life, Love, and a Polar Bear Tattoo* and other books**

"*How to Get Your Book Reviewed* is must reading for every author—regardless of the type of book they write or how they publish their book! Dana Lynn Smith has taken a book marketing tool that many authors ignore and provided a detailed roadmap with hundreds of examples, ideas, and tips."

— **Roger C. Parker, owner of Published and Profitable and author of *99 Questions to Ask Before You Write and Self-Publish Your Brand-Building Book* and other books**

"Dana Lynn Smith reveals insider details in *How to Get Your Book Reviewed*. Tap into this important resource."

— **W. Terry Whalin, author of *Jump Start Your Publishing Dreams* and 60 other books**

# CONTENTS

**Introduction to Book Reviews** .................................................. 1

    What is a Book Review? ......................................................... 1
    How Reviews Sell Books ......................................................... 2
    Is It Worth the Effort? ............................................................. 3
    About This Book .................................................................... 4

**The Book Review Process** ......................................................... 7

    Who Uses Book Reviews for Decision Making ........................... 7
    Where Books Get Reviewed ..................................................... 7
    How the Book Review Process Works ....................................... 8
    Case Study – How Books are Selected for Review .................... 11
    Put Yourself in the Reviewer's Shoes ...................................... 12

**How to Submit Review Copies** ................................................ 15

    Plan Your Review Strategy .................................................... 15
    Decide How Many Review Copies to Distribute ....................... 16
    Select Potential Reviewers ................................................... 17
    Schedule Distribution of Review Copies ................................. 17
    Get Organized .................................................................... 18
    Work with Your Publisher ..................................................... 19
    Prepare Promotional Material ............................................... 19
    Write a Book Announcement Press Release ........................... 20
    Case Study – Sample Press Release ...................................... 21
    Create a Sell Sheet .............................................................. 24
    Prepare Your Online Media Room .......................................... 25
    Sending Queries vs. Sending Books ....................................... 28
    Sending Ebooks vs. Print Books ............................................. 29
    Galleys and Advance Reading Copies ..................................... 31
    Autographing Review Copies ................................................ 32
    How to Ship Review Copies .................................................. 33
    Follow Up ........................................................................... 34

**Potential Pitfalls With Book Reviews** ....................................... 37

    The Self-Publishing Bias ............................................................... 37
    The Ebook Bias ............................................................................. 39
    Times Are Changing...................................................................... 39
    Case Study – The Media is Paying Attention to Self-Published Authors........................................................................................ 40
    Failure to Review.......................................................................... 41
    What Happens to Review Copies of Books .................................. 42
    Review Copies on Amazon ........................................................... 43
    Defacing Review Copies ............................................................... 45
    Dealing With Negative Reviews ................................................... 45
    Common Mistakes in Seeking Book Reviews .............................. 48

## Endorsements, Testimonials and Reviews ................................. 49

    Solicit Endorsements.................................................................... 50
    Case Study – Get High-Profile Endorsements ............................. 56
    Seek a Foreword for Your Nonfiction Book ................................ 58
    Testimonials and Reader Reviews................................................ 59
    Case Study – Ask Loyal Followers to Review Your Book ............ 60
    Take Action................................................................................... 62

## Testimonials and Reviews on Online Bookstores ....................... 63

    Case Study – Do Reviews Really Influence Book Purchases?.... 64
    Actively Solicit Reviews on Online Bookstores .......................... 65
    Case Study – Getting Reviews on Amazon.................................. 67
    Reviews on Amazon.com ............................................................. 68
    Seek Reviews on Amazon............................................................. 70
    Top Amazon Reviewers................................................................ 70
    Amazon Vine Reviewers............................................................... 71
    Research Reviewers of Books Similar to Yours .......................... 72
    Select the Best Potential Reviewers and Find Contact Information .................................................................................. 73
    Update Your Amazon Profile....................................................... 74
    Contact Potential Reviewers on Amazon.................................... 74
    Reviews by Amazon Editors ........................................................ 75
    Amazon Links ............................................................................... 76
    Reviews on BarnesAndNoble.com ............................................... 76

    Other Online Bookstores ............................................................. 78

**Virtual Reader Communities** ..................................................... **79**

    Goodreads .................................................................................... 80
    LibraryThing ................................................................................. 81
    Other Virtual Reader Communities ............................................ 81

**Book Review Blogs** ...................................................................... **87**

    Case Study – The Amanda Hocking Story .................................. 88
    Working With Book Blogs ............................................................ 88
    Finding Book Blogs ...................................................................... 91
    Researching Book Blogs .............................................................. 93
    Estimating the Number of Blog Visitors .................................... 94
    Virtual Book Tours ....................................................................... 95
    Case Study – Do Virtual Book Tours Work? ............................... 96

**Paid Book Reviews** ...................................................................... **99**

    Are Paid Reviews Worth It? ...................................................... 100
    Review Sources ......................................................................... 100

**Book Review Journals** ............................................................... **103**

    The Importance of Reviews to Libraries and Bookstores ........ 103
    Pre-Publication Reviewers ....................................................... 104
    Post-Publication Reviewers ...................................................... 106
    Case Study – Midwest Book Review ........................................ 107
    Working with Review Journals ................................................. 108

**Print Media** ................................................................................ **111**

    Mass Market Newspapers ........................................................ 111
    Case Study – Newspaper Book Reviews .................................. 112
    Literary Magazines and Newspapers ....................................... 113
    Magazines and Newsletters ..................................................... 115
    Researching Media Contacts .................................................... 116
    Tips for Working with the Media ............................................. 117

**Other Book Review Sources** ..................................................... 119

    Create Audio and Video Reviews ............................................. 119
    Offer Review Copies in Publishing Poynters Marketplace ...... 120
    Get Reviews on EzineArticles.com ........................................... 121
    Seek Bloggers to Review Your Book ......................................... 122
    Case Study – Get Bloggers Buzzing About Your Book ............. 122
    A Little Help From Your Friends ............................................... 124
    Check the Book Reviewers List at Writers in the Sky ............. 124
    Enter Book Award Programs .................................................... 124

**Review Other Authors' Books** ..................................................... 129

    How to Write Book Reviews .................................................... 130
    Case Studies – 7 Ways to Write Great Book Reviews ............. 133
    Starting Your Own Review Site ................................................ 134

**How to Use Reviews to Promote Book Sales** ............................ 137

    Where to Post Book Reviews ................................................... 137
    Tips for Using Reviews ............................................................. 139
    Using Reviews on Online Bookstores ...................................... 140
    Case Studies – How Authors Showcase Reviews .................... 141

**About the Author** ........................................................................ 145
**Resources for Authors and Publishers** ..................................... 146

# FOREWORD

*by Ross Rojek, co-founder and editor-in-chief of Sacramento Book Review and other review publications*

I've always been a reader, thanks to my parents. Going to the library every weekend was a major treat. I even kept that up in my teens, biking to the library each weekend, taking back the old books, getting a bag of new ones.

Finding new books to read was easy back then. Find an author you like, read everything they wrote, find another author. New books were judged by their cover, or recommendation from the librarian or the clerk at the Walden Books.

As I got older, I found new books and authors through many of the same sources, yet also started reading reviews of books. Most newspapers had book reviews, if not entire standalone sections. But as the Internet started chewing into newspapers' profit margin, self-publishing and indie publishers also exploded. So as traditional book review outlets cut back, there were even more books to filter through, and more non-traditional outlets talking and reviewing them.

The idea of the *Sacramento Book Review* came after I read *The New York Times* Book Review six weeks running without finding a single book recommended that I was motivated to read. I read a lot, and with pretty broad taste, so not finding anything week after week made me start questioning the editorial selection of the NYTBR. So I started designing in my head MY perfect book review; one that would always have reviews in key subjects. That eventually led to the decision to review a little bit of everything, if not every month, then every other month. Book publishers couldn't understand why we even wanted to try. If the *LA Times* had to cancel their book review, what chance did a book review-only paper in Sacramento have?

But Heidi and I took that leap of faith. Between the two of us, we had most of the skills, or willingness to learn them, to put out a monthly newspaper. And it was quickly embraced by the local literary community. Once when delivering papers and racks for our second issues, a retired librarian working at a Doubleday book store was flipping through the paper while I set up our paper rack. She turned to me and said "We're a big city now. We have a book review."

Part of our success is driven by our origin. We know how hard it is to have a vision and work at getting it done, without help from anyone else. Self-published books get reviewed right next to the best sellers. Our hope is that a reader will be drawn in by a review of a book or author they recognize, but then read a review of something completely new to them and be motivated enough to seek it out.

And we're only one new source of reviews. There are hundreds of blogs and social networks—all talking about books, each with their own focus and voice. And yet there are more new books being published now than ever before.

For a new author with some imagination and determination, this is an exciting time to market their book. Reviews should not only be part of the marketing strategy, but an important one. That first positive review from an "authoritative" source opens one door to the next and brings in some readers who will also go talk about the book with their friends on their social media networks, on the retail website they bought the book, and on book-oriented websites.

# 1
# Introduction to Book Reviews

## What is a Book Review?

With more than 300,000 new books published each year in the U.S. alone, book reviews provide a critical service to booksellers, librarians, and consumers in narrowing down the choices and helping them make good buying decisions.

The term "book review" is commonly used, but there are actually several different types of reviews that can be used to promote books:

- Critical reviews in book journals and mass media
- Reviews from book bloggers, subject matter experts, and other book reviewers
- Customer reviews and testimonials
- Endorsements solicited from experts and high-profile individuals

Traditionally, a book review is a critical review of the content of a book, with the reviewer commenting on the good and bad points of the book.

Many of the reviews posted online these days are really recommendations from readers rather than reviews, but they can be just as effective as traditional reviews. Word of mouth is a powerful selling tool, and websites like Amazon and Goodreads make it easy for readers to share their enthusiasm (or lack of enthusiasm) for the books they read.

## How Reviews Sell Books

Book reviews are a compelling marketing tool for books of all types. Book buyers learn about books by reading reviews in newspapers, consumer magazines, professional journals, newsletters, book review websites, online bookstores, and other blogs and websites.

In addition to bringing books to the attention of potential book buyers, endorsements, testimonials and reviews provide "social proof" that the book is valuable to others, and help the reader determine if the book is a good fit for them.

In fact, reviews are a critical element in any book marketing plan. Here are some examples of the ways that book reviews sell books:

- Expand your marketing reach by getting your book noticed on websites that readers of your genre visit, or in publications read by potential readers for your type of book.
- Positive reviews posted on online bookstores encourage sales once potential customers land on your book page. Reviews can be the tipping point that causes customers to click the buy button.
- Getting reviews from top reviewers on Amazon may also generate traffic to your Amazon page if people click through to look at a particular reviewer's other reviews.

- Good testimonial quotes can be used on your own website and in other promotional materials. You can also extract short quotes from book reviews to use for promotional purposes.
- Bookstore buyers and librarians base many of their ordering decisions on reviews in the major book review journals.
- Good reviews can close the sale for customers who are hesitating about buying your book, or choosing between several similar books.

Of course, it all begins with creating a quality book that will generate both good reviews and satisfied readers.

## Is It Worth the Effort?

There's no guarantee that reviews will translate into sales, but they certainly increase the odds. With the huge amount of competition facing your book, reviews are one of the very best ways to get your book noticed and to influence purchasing decisions of potential customers.

The selling power of reviews makes it well worth the effort. The more reviews you have and the more places your reviews appear, the more exposure and selling power you will have.

You can save time and money and increase your success rate by planning in advance, being selective about where you send review copies, following submission guidelines exactly, and scheduling distribution of your review copies wisely.

Promoting your reviews is also important. After all, it doesn't matter how great your reviews are if people don't see them.

## About This Book

In this book you will learn how to obtain and use various types of book reviews to boost your book sales.

The first section of the book explains the book review process. You will learn:

- How the book review process works
- How books are selected for review
- How, when, and where to submit review copies for maximum effectiveness
- How to create promotional materials to send with review copies
- Potential pitfalls in book reviews and how to avoid them

In the next section you'll learn more about various types of reviews and get details on where to get your books reviewed. Topics covered include:

- Obtaining endorsements
- Getting customer testimonials and reviews
- Harnessing the power of online bookstores
- Using virtual reader communities for reviews and networking
- Getting exposure through book blogs
- The pros and cons of paid review services
- Working with professional book review journals
- Getting reviews and coverage in literary journals, newspapers, magazines, and newsletters
- Using other book review sources
- Promoting your own books by reviewing other authors' books

## Introduction to Book Reviews

In the final chapter, you will learn where and how to use endorsements, testimonials, and reviews for maximum selling power.

Dozens of hyperlinks are included in this book, pointing you to valuable resources and information that will save you time and help you get your book reviewed.

For your convenience, very long URLs have been shortened using http://bit.ly. If you click on a shortened link and it doesn't open, please wait a moment and try again. Sometimes there are temporary glitches on the server.

Web links can change over time. If you spot any broken links, please email me at DanaSmith@TheSavvyBookMarketer.com.

In several places in this book I have included website screenshots. These images are of low resolution because they were made using computer screen-capture software, but they should be useful in illustrating certain points in the text. Now, let's get started with a look at how the book review process works.

# 2

# The Book Review Process

## Who Uses Book Reviews for Decision Making

There are several audiences that use book reviews to make decisions, including:

- Consumers who buy books to read or to give to others.
- Collection development librarians who make purchasing decisions.
- Book distributors who make decisions on which books to represent.
- Retailers who make decisions about which books to stock in their stores.
- Media who may be influenced by reviews when considering whether to give coverage to a book or author.

Keep these various audiences in mind as you plan how to obtain and use your reviews.

## Where Books Get Reviewed

Book reviews appear in a variety of places, such as:

- Book review journals and literary journals
- Newspapers, magazines, newsletters, and other publications
- Book blogs, topical blogs, and other websites
- Online bookstores
- Virtual reader communities like Goodreads and LibraryThing
- Author and publisher websites and promotional materials

In addition, endorsements, testimonials, and excerpts from reviews are used on book covers, on promotional pages within books, and in other book promotion material.

Later chapters in this book give more details on each of these types of reviews, but in this chapter we will discuss in general how the review process works.

## Savvy Tip

It's best to concentrate your efforts on getting reviews in places that reach lots of readers and are closely aligned with the topic or audience of your book. But don't discount low traffic sites completely. Having a review on a website or blog with low traffic will not reach many readers, but it may generate backlinks to your website and testimonial quotes to use on your website and marketing materials.

## How the Book Review Process Works

Authors and publishers send their books to reviewers in hopes of getting a review or endorsement, which will help bring the book to the attention of more people and persuade potential customers that the book is a good fit for them.

In this section, we will look specifically at the review process for publications and websites that review books on a regular basis. It's important to remember that a book reviewer's responsibility is to the readers of their reviews, not to the author or publisher. Reviewers aren't really in the business of helping authors further their careers or helping publishers sell more books. Their goal is to help readers (and librarians, booksellers, distributors, etc.) make appropriate book selections.

Here is a basic overview of the process:

1. Authors and publishers research potential reviewers and send books (or queries) to those review outlets that are a match for their book, in terms of subject matter and the reviewer's guidelines. It's the author or publisher's responsibility to make sure the book is a good fit, send appropriate materials with the book, and package it to arrive safely.

2. Reviewers have no obligation to review every book submitted to them, and each reviewer has his or her own criteria (which may be both objective and subjective) for deciding which books to select and review. Even if a reviewer has expressed interest in a book in response to a query, that's no guarantee that a review will be published. Sometimes reviewers are just too overwhelmed to get to all of the books they intend to review, or they may find upon receipt that the book is not of sufficient quality to merit a review.

3. Once the review is published, the reviewer should send the publisher a link (if it's online) or a tear sheet (if it's in print.) Some reviewers also post their reviews on sites such as Amazon.com, although there is no obligation to do so.

It's unrealistic to expect to get a response from everyone to whom you send a review copy. Also, not all books that are assigned to a reviewer will actually get a published review. Sometimes the reviewer fails to do the review, or the editor feels the review was not up to the organization's standards. Also, some sites and publications do not publish negative reviews, so a review may be scrapped because the reviewer could not find enough merit in the book to do a positive review.

Here are some of the most common reasons that books are not assigned to a reviewer or not reviewed:

**Time or space constraints** – Most publications and websites that review books regularly have the time and space to review only a small percentage of the submissions received.

**Poor quality** – If the quality of the writing or editing, or the quality of the publication (book cover, interior, printing) are not up to professional standards, a book is likely to end up in the reject pile. Sometimes the quality of the writing and editing isn't clear until the reviewer has already started reading the book.

**Not a good fit** – Some authors and publishers don't do enough research to determine if their book is appropriate for the reviewer. The book's subject matter or its format (galley vs. finished book), may not fit with the reviewer's editorial policies.

**Poor communication** – Sometimes authors or publishers fail to follow clearly stated review guidelines, provide inadequate marketing materials or contact information, or are just generally pushy or annoying.

**Problem reviewers** – Some people claim to be book reviewers in order to get free books for reading or re-sale, while others may have good intentions but do not follow through after agreeing to review a book.

In the case study below, Jim Cox shares a real-life view of what it's like to be on the receiving end of review copies.

## Case Study – How Books are Selected for Review

*by Jim Cox, Editor-in-Chief, Midwest Book Review, reprinted with permission.*

Let's say that your book has arrived on the reviewer's desk in this morning's mail along with 49 others. The reviewer (or the review editor) will be doing a kind of literary triage and separating those 50 newly arrived books into three categories:

1. **Immediate Discards**

This is anything that at first glance is deemed thematically inappropriate; poorly packaged; a galley where the finished copy is required/a finished copy where a galley is required; from a small press when only major houses are considered; a missing or poorly written publicity release; the reviewer just did reviews on a title too similar to the one that is now presented to their attention; reviewer bias, prejudice, or just having a bad hair day.

2. **Immediate Assignments**

It's a terrific looking book; it's a high-profile author; it just happens to be a subject that the reviewer is currently writing his or her column on; the accompanying publicity release is a real "grabber" and compelling; the editor has a specific reviewer in mind who would be thrilled to review this particular title because it's in their particular area of interest, hobby or profession.

3. **A Possible for Later Assignment**

It's thematically appropriate; the publicity release is okay; there may be a reviewer or a column coming up in the near future that it might fit; (and in the case of editors like myself doing the triage) I might be able to talk one of my reviewers into accepting the assignment.

## Put Yourself in the Reviewer's Shoes

As you plan your book review strategy and marketing materials, it's helpful to put yourself in the reviewer's shoes. Here are some things to consider:

- Book review journals and other major media receive thousands of books a year and can only review a small percentage of them. Opening, sorting and disposing of this huge volume of books can be a daunting task (one that is often assigned to interns).

- Reviewers receive many books that are not appropriate for the website or publication, have not been submitted in accordance with their review policies, or are not professionally produced. It's frustrating for the reviewers to have to deal with these books—they consume both time and space.

- Your potential reviewers are most likely very busy people. Remember that you are asking for a favor, be gracious, and do everything that you can to make it easy for the person to help you.

- Newspapers and magazines are shrinking due to competition from online media and lower ad revenue. Find a way to make your book relevant, and also look for coverage beyond the book review section.

- Book reviewers are avid readers, but many of them receive no compensation other than a copy of the book. Consider your book a gift to the reviewer, to be used as they see fit.

- Reading and writing a book review is a time consuming process, and most reviewers have many other demands on their time, including paying jobs and family. These folks are working really hard to share their love of books with others. Be considerate of them and their time.

- Book bloggers not only devote their time to reading and reviewing books, they also must create and maintain a website, and post reviews and other content on the site. They must pay for web hosting and other expenses, and most book blogs generate little or no income.

Now that you have a better understanding of the review process, in the next chapter we will discuss the mechanics of planning your review strategy and sending out review copies.

# 3

# How to Submit Review Copies

## Plan Your Review Strategy

The first step to success is to develop a strategy for your reviews. Here are some tips:

- Consider your goals and your book's target audiences.
- Set a budget and decide how many books you can send out.
- Put together a list of potential reviewers, arranged by the categories covered in this book.
- Prioritize your list, identifying the most important prospects.
- Develop a schedule, considering the deadlines of pre-publication reviewers.
- Get organized—set up a spreadsheet or other tracking device.
- Prepare good promotional materials.
- Order your galleys or review copies in plenty of time and allow time for mailing.

## Decide How Many Review Copies to Distribute

There's no easy answer to the question of how many review copies to send out. How much money you should spend on review copies (and book promotion in general) depends in part on the type of book you have published, the sales potential of the book, and your own goals and budget.

Here are some things to keep in mind as you consider your budget:

- Calculate the total cost per review copy, including the cost of printing and shipping the book to you, the cost of the envelope and printed materials to be enclosed, and the postage cost to mail to reviewers.

- Not all review copies will result in a review, testimonial or endorsement, so you will need to send out quite a few copies to get significant results. It's hard to say what your success rate will be, but it will probably vary for different types of potential reviewers. You will probably have a higher success rate with people who already know you or know your reputation.

- Review copies are an investment that could pay off in a big way. For example, just one good review in a widely read publication such as *Library Journal* could result in hundreds or thousands of sales.

- Although you will probably distribute most of your review copies in the first few months of a book's life, budget for extra books to send later as opportunities arise.

## Select Potential Reviewers

In the later chapters of this book you will learn about several different types of reviewers where you can submit review copies. It's really important to do your homework and make sure that you are selecting prospects that are a good fit for your particular book.

As you compile your review list, make sure that you have correct contact information (including email, phone number and postal mail, if possible) and that you have the right contact person, with the name spelled correctly.

In some cases, you may want to study the style and tone of other book reviews that have been published by the prospective reviewer that you are considering. While most good reviewers provide fair and balanced reviews, some have a tendency to be rather harsh or to let their personal views color their reviews.

When researching publications or websites that do not review books on a regular basis, it's a good idea to find out if they ever do book reviews and who handles them. When contacting someone who has written a review of a similar book, you can let them know that you enjoyed their review of that book and you thought that they might also enjoy your book.

## Schedule Distribution of Review Copies

Once you have made a list of potential reviewers, plan your schedule to get review copies to the reviewers at the optimum time.

For example, pre-publication book review journals want to receive galleys at least three months before the publication date. Some publications want to see the book immediately after publication. Some reviewers will review books for up to a year after publication. Ideally, you should contact potential endorsers several months before the book is printed.

You may want to spread out some of your review copies over a period of several months to make it easier on you and to have an ongoing supply of new reviews to promote.

It is a good idea to get some reviews onto Amazon as soon as possible so that shoppers on the site will be able to see positive feedback on the book. But getting reviews in online bookstores is an ongoing process that will last for the life of the book.

## Get Organized

A spreadsheet program like Excel is ideal for keeping track of your review plan. You can set up a separate tab or file for each category of reviewer (as outlined in this book), and then create columns for details such as the reviewer's name, contact information, submission requirements, date sent, etc.

People and organizations that review books regularly (such as book review blogs and review journals) usually have their submission requirements posted on their website. **The importance of reading and following those instructions cannot be emphasized enough.** Publishers who do not follow the instructions are wasting their time and money and the reviewer's time. Submission guidelines may specify what types of books are accepted, whether a query should be sent first, how many copies to send, what to enclose with the book, and where to ship the book. If there are no guidelines, it's best to query before spending money to send a book.

## Work with Your Publisher

If you have a traditional publisher, their publicist will most likely be sending out the pre-publication galleys and some other review copies. Speak to the publicist early on about their plans and ask for a list of every place a review copy will be sent. Make it clear that you want to support and supplement the publisher's efforts. Ask if you can add additional names to their review list or obtain some review copies to send out on your own. It doesn't hurt to stay in touch with the publicist to make sure that review copies have been sent out (publicists may be juggling a number of different books) but don't come across as too demanding.

Remember that subsidy publishers (self-publishing companies) do not do any promotion – you are on your own in handling your reviews.

## Prepare Promotional Material

Many authors create lovely media kits to send along with their review copies. Unfortunately, in larger organizations the packages are opened in the mail room (or by interns) and the reviewer may never see the media kit. However, the person who makes decisions about assigning books for review may see the media kit, depending on the organization.

In cases where the book is likely to get passed on to another person for review (book review journals, media, book bloggers with multiple reviewers) you can also attach an overview to the inside front cover of the book with a small piece of tape, listing a synopsis or benefits, target audience, a brief note on your platform and marketing plans, and your contact information. On pre-publication galleys, this information is often printed on the back cover.

Common marketing pieces mailed with review copies include a press release, a sell sheet, and perhaps an author bio. If you're sending a book to someone who does not review books as their main business, also include a cover letter. Some publishers include a full media kit with their review copies, including items such as press clippings, interview questions, fact sheets, and author photos. You might want to include these additional materials for certain reviewers.

## Savvy Tip

Make sure that your name and contact information (email, phone number and postal address) are clearly visible on at least one (preferably all) of the printed materials that you send with the book, and in any query letters that you send.

Below are more details on how to create the press release and the sell sheet.

## Write a Book Announcement Press Release

Some review submission guidelines specify that a press release should be sent with the book, and it's a good idea to send one with all review copies. Reviewers often read the release in making a decision to review the book, but it is also valuable for another purpose. Some media, who have very limited time for reading books and writing reviews, will quote directly from the press release in their review. So, make sure your release is as good as it can be — something that you would be proud to see reprinted in a review.

The basic elements of a book announcement press release are:

- Contact information (name, email, phone)
- Headline (and perhaps a subhead)
- Lead – one or two sentences, including the book title

- Book description – a little longer description of the book, its target audiences and how it benefits readers. You may want to include some bullet points to illustrate features/benefits of the book. For a novel, you would include the synopsis of the book.
- Quote from the author or publisher
- Author bio/credentials
- Book details – repeat title and price and state where it's available

Press releases should be brief – try to keep it one page. You want to provide an enticing description of the book, but don't resort to hype. You can probably pull much of the descriptive copy from the back cover of your book.

In the book description paragraph, it's customary to include a statement in parenthesis listing the price, publisher name, and publication date. For example:

*Facebook Guide for Authors* ($15, Texana Publishing, April, 2011).

## Case Study – Sample Press Release

The sample press release below is courtesy of Sandra Beckwith. Her workbook, *Build Book Buzz Publicity Forms and Templates*, features fill-in-the-blank templates and samples for various types of press releases and publicity materials, along with instructions on how to use them. Book publicity resources: http://bit.ly/PublicityResources

*FOR IMMEDIATE RELEASE*

CONTACT: Courtney Goethals, 800-555-1212, name@mail.com

## New Guide Helps Nonprofits Stretch Marketing Dollars for Maximum Publicity

Nonprofits Can Finally Capture Essential Media Attention

CHICAGO, IL — date — A new book from an award-winning publicist helps nonprofit organizations large and small discover and use the tools and techniques that will help transform them into high-profile media darlings.

In *Publicity for Nonprofits: Generating Media Exposure That Leads to Awareness, Growth, and Contributions*, ($23.95 Kaplan Publishing, June 20XX) author Sandra Beckwith taps her 25 years of hands-on publicity know-how to outline successful media relations strategies tailored for nonprofit organizations. This detailed, step-by-step guide includes examples of press releases, op-ed essays, pitch letters, public service announcements and other important outreach tools.

This timely and practical guide doesn't just explain why publicity is important – it shows how to use cost-effective publicity plans and tactics to reach fundraising goals, educate and influence consumers, and recruit employees and volunteers. In *Publicity for Nonprofits: Generating Media Exposure That Leads to Awareness, Growth, and Contributions*, Beckwith offers fascinating case studies, detailed instructions, and a rich array of publicity tools and tactics that will help nonprofit organizations learn how to:

- Create an affordable publicity plan that integrates goals, objectives, and key strategies
- Determine which tools and tactics will have the most impact on the organization's goals

- Develop and pitch newsworthy stories with powerful messages that will capture media attention and resonate with audiences
- Maximize the publicity potential of an organization's activities, talents and resources

"When I speak to nonprofit groups about publicity, they are never interested in theory," says Beckwith. "They want to know how to do it – what tools and tactics will get them the farthest? Which approach will have the greatest impact with the least amount of expense? When is a press conference a good idea and when is not the best choice for communicating information? I wrote this book to give them the answers and information they need to succeed in a highly-competitive, increasingly complex media world."

**Sandra Beckwith** has more than 25 years of award-winning public relations experience. A recipient of the coveted Silver Anvil Award from the Public Relations Society of America, her public relations background includes assignments at one of the world's largest public relations firms and a large national consumer products company. Now a consultant who helps others learn how to generate their own publicity, her clients include several nonprofit organizations.

*Publicity for Nonprofits: Generating Media Exposure that Leads to Awareness, Growth, and Contributions* ($23.95, 256 pages, 7 ¼ x 9, paperback, ISBN: 1-4195-2299-X) is available at neighborhood and online booksellers or by calling 800-245-BOOK.

Kaplan Publishing is one of the nation's leading education, career and business publishers. Kaplan Publishing, with offices in New York and Chicago, produces more than 150 books a year on test preparation, admissions, academic and professional development, general business, management, sales, marketing, real estate, finance and investing. Kaplan Publishing is a unit of Kaplan, Inc., a wholly owned subsidiary of The Washington Post Company (NYSE: WPO). For more information, please visit www.kaplanpublishing.com.

## Create a Sell Sheet

In addition to the press release, I recommend enclosing a marketing piece that summarizes everything the potential reviewer needs to know about your book. Publishers often create a one-page flyer called a sell sheet for marketing purposes, and this works well for sending with review copies. Even if the reviewer requests a press release about the book, I suggest including the sell sheet too. You can also include a downloadable PDF version on your website.

The sell sheet should include a book cover, description (essentially the back cover copy from the book explaining the premise, target market and benefits of the book, or a synopsis for a novel), and a brief author bio. Other items commonly included are:

- Endorsements and testimonial quotes
- Book awards or writing awards
- Publication date
- List price
- Size, format, and page count (and shipping weight if you're selling to bookstores)
- ISBN and LCCN numbers
- Book wholesaler availability
- Publisher name
- Special features in the book
- Contact information for the author and/or publisher

Some sell sheets are designed by graphic artists, but you may want to consider designing your own sell sheet in Microsoft Word, Publisher, or another program so that you can easily update it with new testimonial quotes, book awards, etc. as you receive them. You can create a two column format or use text boxes to place elements on the page. Consult the Word help menu or search online to learn how to use text boxes.

You can print sell sheets on your own printer or send the file to a local copy shop to be digitally printed on slightly coated paper. If you use your own printer, buy "color copy paper" or a similar paper that will make better looking prints than plain copy paper.

## Prepare Your Online Media Room

All authors and publishers need a blog or website for promotional purposes. While that topic is beyond the scope of this book, keep in mind that it's important to set up a media room on your site before you start sending out review copies or doing other promotions.

## Savvy Tip

When sending queries or review copies to prospective reviewers and endorsers, it's a good idea to include a link to your online media room where prospects can learn more about you and your book.

Below are some tips for creating your own media room.

The goal of an online media room is to make it easy for reviewers, journalists, talk show producers, and other influencers to quickly find everything they need to know about you and your book.

Online author and book publicity pages are called by several names, including media room, media kit, press room or press kit, or they are simply labeled as Media or Press on the site's navigation menu. On some sites, the media page is accessed through a link from the About page of the site. Whatever you call your book publicity page, just make sure it's clearly marked and easy to find from any page on your site.

Remember, your media page isn't just for the media – it's a great place to showcase your credentials and biographic information for other author and book publicity purposes. For example, you can link to your media page when introducing yourself to reviewers, bloggers, potential clients and potential partners.

Here are some of the most important elements to include on your media page. If this is too much information for one page, you can create links to additional pages from the main media page.

- **About the Author** – You might create two bios, a short one of about three sentences (imagine a radio announcer introducing you) and another bio about half a page long.
- **About the Book** – Summary of your book, written in a news style without marketing hype.
- **Praise/Endorsements/Reviews** – Feature any celebrity quotes prominently.
- **Awards** – Book awards and writing awards received by the author.
- **Author Photos** – High resolution version for print and low resolution for online use. Include a caption beneath your photo listing your credentials or author tagline.
- **Book Covers** – High resolution for print and low resolution for online use.

- **Contact Information** – Make this easy to find and include email address, phone number, and mailing address, if applicable. See these tips for displaying and protecting your email address online: http://bit.ly/xpi2nn

Other elements commonly found on author and book publicity pages include:

- **Complete Press Kit** – One page or document containing all of your media information in one place.
- **In the Media** – Provide links to previous media coverage that you've received. If you have appeared in any major print or broadcast media, include their logos prominently on your media page.
- **Audio and/or Video Clips** – Short audio or video clips of you (preferably being interviewed) allow potential interviewers to hear or see you in action. You can also include your book video trailer or audio trailer.
- **Interview Topics** – A list of topics you can speak about.
- **Sample Q & A** – Radio stations, in particular, will appreciate using questions you provide for an interview.
- **Article Topics** – A list of topics you can write about and/or suggested angles for feature stories about you. You might even provide pre-written stories or tips for the media to use.
- **Fact Sheet** – One-page document with pertinent facts about your industry or book topic.
- **Press Releases** – Links to online versions of press releases about you, your book or business.
- **Media References** – Nice quotes from media who have interviewed you or worked with you.

- **Clients Include** – If you're a consultant, you might want to post a list of important clients (with their permission) and a few testimonial quotes from clients.

Many online book publicity pages contain downloadable documents in PDF format, but some publicists advise just putting the text of your media materials on a Web page and letting people copy and paste from there. Even when it's convenient to copy or download your book publicity materials from your website, some people will still want you to email information to them or even send a printed media kit.

## Sending Queries vs. Sending Books

The cost of sending out review copies can really add up. To save money, you may want to send queries to at least some of your prospects first, rather than sending a book, to determine their interest. But keep in mind that a query (especially an email) is easier to overlook or ignore than a package with a book in it.

Book review journals will want a copy of the book. I think that sending a book is probably best for most other media because they are less likely to respond to a query. And don't forget the old-fashioned phone call—it can be effective with potential endorsers and some media.

For book review blogs, be sure to read the submission instructions. Many of them will state whether they prefer to receive queries or books, and it's important to follow their instructions.

It's best to send a printed book to your most important potential endorsers and reviewers.

For some reviewers, you may want to email a query and a sample chapter or two (or a link where people can download samples online). Keep your query brief. Here are some suggestions on what to include:

- Explain why you are contacting this person (how you know of them, why you think they are an ideal person to review your book, etc.)
- Describe exactly what you want (review in their blog, endorsement, etc.)
- Include brief (one or two paragraphs) synopsis or overview of the book and its target market.
- Attach a PDF with a few sample chapters (or the entire book), or provide a link to an online page where people can download the samples. For media and larger organizations, it's probably better to include a link rather than sending an attachment. Many people are wary of clicking on attached documents, especially Word documents, for fear of computer viruses. If you do send attachments, be sure to save your file as a PDF. (Click Save As and select PDF as the file type.)
- Let them know that you will be happy to send a printed book if they are interested.
- Thank the prospect.

## Sending Ebooks vs. Print Books

These days, many people prefer to read on their Kindle or other mobile device. Make it easy on your prospective endorsers and reviewers by offering your manuscript or finished book in several ebook formats, including mobi or prc (for Kindle) epub (for most other e-readers) and PDF.

One way to do that is to make your book available for sale on Smashwords.com, then give reviewers a coupon for a 100% discount. From your Smashwords account dashboard, select **Generate and Manage Other Coupons** in the left column to create a coupon.

The downside of offering review copies through Smashwords is that reviewers may find it inconvenient to go through the several steps necessary to redeem their coupon for a free book, and they will have to set up a user name and password if they don't already have a Smashwords account. You might want to include a few tips on downloading from Smashwords for those who are not familiar with the site. For example:

- Click the Add to Cart link near the upper right of the screen.

- Enter Coupon code and click Update.

- Click the green Checkout button and you will see a confirmation page.

- Double click the link with the book name, then scroll down to click on the Download link next to the ebook format of your choice.

- If you need help transferring ebooks to your ebook reading device, see this page:

    https://www.smashwords.com/about/supportfaq#devices

(Double check these instructions to make sure they work before you give them to anyone!)

Learn more about publishing on Smashwords at www.SavvyEbookPublishing.com

"You can also distribute ebook review copies by giving them as a gift through the Kindle or Nook stores," points out Phyllis Zimbler Miller, author of the novels *Mrs. Lieutenant* and *Lt. Commander Mollie Sanders*.

"Just click the Give as a Gift button. Of course, you will have to pay for the ebook, but you will get part of the cost back in royalties and it will chalk up one more sale to your account. Plus, it's easier and cheaper than mailing a printed book," she adds.

Another option is to create a review copy page on your website and upload several ebook formats to that page so that reviewers can download them. Make this page hidden from search engines.

Or simply upload each version of the book to a server somewhere and provide links to those files online. For example, you can email the file to yourself using a file transfer service such as YouSendIt.com and then direct people to the download link that YouSendIt provides. Or save the files to an online file storage service such as Amazon Cloud Drive. Learn more about Amazon Cloud Drive at:
 www.amazon.com/clouddrive/learnmore

Always offer to send a printed copy of the book if the potential reviewer prefers.

## Galleys and Advance Reading Copies

Pre-publication reviewers expect to receive a galley (often called an uncorrected proof, advance reading copy, or ARC) because the book is not yet printed three months prior to publication when the reviewers want to look at it. This is a bound copy of the almost finished book, which still may be in the final proofreading stages.

Traditionally, galleys have plain white covers, rather than the finished book cover. On the front cover is printed the book title, author name and publisher name. The spine contains the title, author, publisher, and publication date. The back cover may contain the publication date, a few early endorsements, and a brief overview of the book marketing plan.

Usually advance reading copies (ARCs) submitted to reviewers have the real cover on the book, although space may have been left on the cover to insert endorsements. There are several printers that specialize in producing galleys and ARCs, or you can get them printed through a print-on-demand printer such as Lulu.com.

Ideally, the final book cover will contain endorsements and review excerpts that have been obtained during the final stages of production.

## Autographing Review Copies

When sending printed books, many authors like to autograph their books, perhaps including the name of the person they are sending the book to.

Put yourself in the reviewer's shoes – they may receive dozens (or even hundreds) of books a month and they cannot keep them all. The books have to be disposed of somehow. Review copies may be sold at used bookstores or Amazon Marketplace (more on that in Chapter 4), donated to libraries or schools, or given to friends. Some reviewers list their policy on their website.

My advice is to be selective about how you autograph books. I suggest doing an autograph and personal note for people that you know, people who have given you an endorsement or have done you a favor, or people who are closely tied to the subject matter of the book – anyone who might have a personal reason to keep the book or value your personal note.

For most other review copies, I would simply sign your name on the title page, perhaps with a generic greeting such as "warm wishes" or some other phrase related to the topic of the book. This is a nice gesture, but does not detract from the book if the reviewer shares, donates or sells it.

## How to Ship Review Copies

First, you'll need to decide what sort of container to send your review copies in. Remember that it has to be large enough to hold the book and any printed materials you are sending with it. Plain envelopes are least expensive, but the book might be damaged in transit. Envelopes that are padded with bubble wrap or paper offer better protection. Cardboard mailers are another option.

Compare prices at your local discount store, warehouse store, and office supply store. If you are going to be sending out a lot of review copies (and/or fulfilling book orders yourself) also check the prices at a shipping supply company such as Uline.com.

The U.S. Postal Service is usually the least expensive way to ship single copies of books. Weigh your entire package (envelope, book, printed materials), then check the website at USPS.gov to calculate the cost of Media Mail vs. First Class postage. Media Mail (used to mail books and other media) is the cheapest, but delivery can sometimes take one to three weeks. First Class is generally faster and more reliable. If your package is unusually heavy or you are in a hurry, you might use Priority Mail instead.

Or you can take your package to the post office to be weighed and speak to the clerk about your mailing options and costs.

Books do get lost in the mail sometimes, and that may be more likely for books sent via Media Mail. If you want to verify that your review copies have been received, the post office can supply a proof of delivery or return receipt for an additional fee.

If you have quite a few review copies to package and mail, consider inviting some friends over to help you and make it a party!

Make sure that you have the right person's name (spelled correctly) and correct mailing address and also include your full return address on the package including your name and company name (pre-printed stickers are ideal.)

Keep in mind that mailrooms in some organizations (such as mass media) are wary of incoming packages, and also many of the people you talk to won't remember speaking to you. If you have queried prospective reviewers beforehand, you can increase the chances of them getting and opening the package by writing a note on the outside. Here's an example:

*Material requested by John Moore – enclosed is the How to Get Your Book Reviewed book that we discussed by phone on 7/6/11.*

## Follow Up

When sending queries, it's a good idea to follow up in about a week if you haven't received a reply. The same goes for review copies—call or email the prospect in about seven to ten days to make sure the book was received, and ask if the reviewer plans to do a review and when it might be published. A second or third follow up contact might be needed, but the last thing you want to do is be annoying or sound demanding.

Most book review journals and book bloggers receive a large number of books and they may not have time to answer inquiries about whether they received your book or they are going to review it. Remember that book bloggers are often single-person volunteer operations. They may even have a statement in their review guidelines that they do not welcome such inquiries. If so, respect their wishes.

Of course, following up means having an organized list of when and where your review copies have been sent and what contacts you have made with each person or organization, so be sure to keep good records. You will also need to make sure that you receive a copy of (or link to) each review that was done.

# 4
# Potential Pitfalls With Book Reviews

Authors and publishers devote considerable time and expense in sending out review copies of their books, in hopes of generating reviews and boosting sales. But there are several potential pitfalls in dealing with book reviews.

## The Self-Publishing Bias

If you have independently published your book or published through a subsidy publisher (self-publishing company), you are likely to find that many (or most) reviewers are biased against self-published books. Some reviewers state in their submission guidelines that they do not accept self-published books. Some even state "no POD books," which is a misnomer, since print-on-demand is a printing method used by all types of publishers.

It's helpful to try to understand some of the reasons behind this bias.

- Perhaps the reviewers are simply so overwhelmed with book submissions that they are using a "no self-published books" policy to narrow down the number of books to consider for review.

- Maybe the reviewer's readers have conveyed that they prefer to read reviews of books from mainstream publishers or books that are available in bookstores.

- There could be a misconception that self-publishing is a last resort for books that aren't good enough to be bought by traditional publishing houses.

- Maybe the reviewer has seen so many badly written and produced books that they assume that most self-published books are poorly done.

- For journals that cater to bookstores (such as *Publishers Weekly*) it doesn't make sense to review books published through subsidy publishers, because bookstores generally won't sell them.

If you are self-published, it's important to produce a quality product and present your book in the most professional light possible. While it's true that there are many poor quality books, there are also many excellent self-published books that are well written, edited and designed, and these deserve the attention of reviewers. There are even some book review blogs that openly welcome self-published books.

The thorny question is whether you should submit to some blogs or publications that have a "no self-published books" rule. There's no easy answer, but my advice is to pick your battles. If your book is professionally produced and you feel that it's a good fit for a particular reviewer, go ahead and submit it. (Yes, I know that's bending the rule about following submission guidelines – don't get carried away!) Just realize that it may be a long shot.

Opinions differ on how to present self-published books to reviewers. Some people recommend making no mention of the fact that the book is self-published, while others say that there's no need to try to hide the fact that a book is self-published. In general, I'd say it's best to make no mention of self-publishing and just concentrate on finding reviewers that are the best fit for the type of book you published. An exception to that is in cases where you feel that being self-published will actually give you an advantage, such as with Midwest Book Review, with book blogs that are openly friendly to self-published books, or with media who seem open to self-published authors.

*"Regardless of the deep-seated sentiments of the mainstream reviewers, self-published authors can get reviews from the major review journals. And it's definitely worth the effort."*

Fern Reiss
CEO of PublishingGame.com

## The Ebook Bias

Authors who publish exclusively in ebook format also face challenges. Many mainstream reviewers won't accept ebooks for review and many book awards programs do not accept ebooks. If you publish ebooks only, you will need to do some additional research to find sites that will accept ebooks.

## Times Are Changing

The good news is that the bias against self-published books and ebook only books is slowly fading, especially among online reviewers and some media. The spectacular success of independent authors like John Locke, Amanda Hocking and J.A. Konrath in selling vast numbers of Kindle books has helped to prove that traditional publishers are not required for big sales and that ebooks are "real" books. The rapid rate of growth for ebook sales also helps to legitimize them.

The trends in independent publishing and ebook sales are capturing the interest of the media, and major newspapers like *The New York Times* and the *Wall Street Journal* have covered these stories. You might look for ways to capitalize on these trends in getting your own media coverage.

## Case Study – The Media is Paying Attention to Self-Published Authors

by Terry Tracy, author of *A Great Place for a Seizure*.

I attended a book reading shortly after my book was published. I arrived early to get a chance to talk with the author and stayed a while afterward and asked her for advice. Then she started asking me more questions about my novel. At the end of our conversation, she asked me if I would be willing to be interviewed as part of a series that she is producing for BBC radio on 60 authors, established and new. Those 59 other authors include J.K. Rowling and Dan Brown. I made it clear to her that I was self-published but she was still interested, which took me by surprise.

Lesson Learned: The stigma of self-publishing as a sign of a writer's failure is a view that is fading. Self-published authors are being perceived as innovative pioneers willing to challenge the system. If a self-published author has a quality book (well-written and without typos) with a worthwhile message, the big, traditional media is willing to listen because right now, being self-published IS the story.

Some self-publishing manuals will tell you to try to hide the fact that you are self-published when you are marketing. I think we should be honest and open about self-publishing. Don't let the fact of being self-published hinder your pride in your book, nor your press strategy.

## Failure to Review

Use caution when sending review copies to individuals who request them. Some people claim to be book reviewers as a way to get free books either for reading or for re-sale. Most legitimate reviewers don't solicit review copies.

If you don't know much about a reviewer who requests a book, it's a good idea to politely inquire what other book reviews they have done and where they were published, and ask to see copies of some of their reviews.

If an expert in your book's subject matter inquires about a review copy, it's usually a good idea to send it. You can word your response to convey that you are happy to send them a complimentary review copy of the book and you would be very grateful for their feedback. Don't be afraid to follow up in a few weeks and ask what they thought of the book. Getting an endorsement or review from a leading expert could be quite valuable.

Some people who request review copies (or respond to your queries) have good intentions, but simply won't find the time to write and post a book review. Many legitimate reviewers are simply overwhelmed with books and cannot get to all of the ones they want to review.

*"I sent copies of my book to book bloggers who responded to my email that they indeed wanted to review the book, but who never reviewed it. I later realized that I wasn't anyone to them, so my book got buried in the avalanche of books they receive.*

*I found that bloggers on my virtual book tour and book reviewers whom I connected with through social media were much more committed to actually reviewing my book."*

Phyllis Zimbler Miller, MillerMosaicLLC.com

Also, keep in mind that if you have sent books to people who did not request them, there is no reason to "expect" a review. Only a certain percentage of reviewers that you approach will actually review the book.

## What Happens to Review Copies of Books

The issue of how reviewers dispose of the books that are sent to them can be controversial.

It's important to understand that professional reviewers receive hundreds or thousands of books a year, and they have to do something with all of those books. Also, keep in mind that authors and publishers send out free copies of their books in hopes of getting something of value (a book review) in return. Review copies become the property of the person or organization that received them and they are entitled to dispose of them however they see fit.

In organizations such as book review journals and mass media outlets, the individual reviewers usually get to keep the books that are assigned to them for review. In many cases, the book is their only form of compensation. The books that are not reviewed are disposed of in some way. Employees may be allowed to select the ones they want to take home, or the books may be donated to libraries, schools or other nonprofit organizations. In some cases, books may be sold through a used bookstore or online bookstore, or even thrown in the trash or recycling bin.

Many books that are donated to libraries end up being sold in their book sale fundraisers, rather than being placed into circulation. Individual book reviewers can only keep so many books and eventually they have to dispose of them somehow, usually through donation or sale (or giving them to friends, who will eventually dispose of them.) When employees of the review organizations take books home, they may be re-selling the books right away, or they may read them first and then dispose of them (or give them to friends.)

Many authors and publishers have no problem with books being donated to schools or libraries or given to friends. After all, the more people who read a book, the more chance of word-of-mouth publicity and even customer reviews on sites like Amazon and Goodreads. People who enjoy a free copy of a book may also purchase some of the author's other books.

Most in the publishing industry agree that selling galleys (which are essentially unfinished books still in the proofreading stage and without proper covers) is unethical. But the practice of selling ARCs and finished books remains highly controversial, especially when the books are offered for sale on the Amazon Marketplace.

## Review Copies on Amazon

It's disheartening for authors to see their review copies being sold on Amazon for a fraction of the regular list price, and knowing that they will receive no royalty or payment for those sales.

Amazon's policies do prohibit the sale of advance reading copies and galleys, although it's not completely clear whether the policy extends to regular printed copies of books. Here's an excerpt from their policies at http://amzn.to/oquYlU.

*"Promotional versions of media products, including books (advance reading copies and uncorrected proofs), music, and videos (screeners) are prohibited. These products are distributed for promotional consideration and generally are not authorized for retail distribution or sale."*

If you want to spend the time and effort to contact Amazon you may be able to get your ARCs and galleys removed from the Amazon Marketplace, and perhaps finished books that have been marked as review copies.

However, it's helpful to consider whether the review copies for sale on Amazon are really hurting sales of your books. Many Amazon shoppers pay no attention to the Marketplace offers. Either they are not interested in buying from individuals, they don't even notice the Marketplace offers, or they may want to combine several purchases to get free shipping from Amazon when their order totals $25 or more.

People who do buy from the Marketplace may be bargain seekers who would not have paid full price, or they might recommend the book to a friend, buy your other books, or leave a nice review on Amazon.

If you aren't familiar with the Amazon Marketplace, here's what a typical book listing looks like on Amazon:

If you click on the "16 new from $10.95" link you will be taken to the Amazon Marketplace page listing new copies of this book available for sale by book dealers and individuals. Keep in mind that many of these listings are from book dealers who don't actually have the book – they will order it from Ingram if they get an order. Clicking on the "7 used from $10.39" link takes you to the Amazon Marketplace page where people are selling used copies of this book.

## Defacing Review Copies

Some authors and publishers attempt to stop the practice of selling review copies by defacing the books in some way, usually by using stickers or stamps that say something like "Review Copy – Not for Resale." Some even damage the book by doing something like clipping the corners off the covers.

In general, defacing review copies is considered bad form, and in many cases it doesn't stop people from trying to re-sell the books. Some individual reviewers object to this practice so much that they won't even review books that have been defaced.

Consider that many reviewers are avid readers who truly love books and they hate to see books defaced. And remember that the book is the only compensation that many reviewers get for writing and posting a review, so it's not really fair to deprive them of being able to dispose of the book in the manner that they see fit, whether it's giving the book to a friend, donating it to their library, or selling it.

If you feel that you must mark your review copies in some way, consider stamping them on the inside front cover or the title page, rather than on the outside or page edges.

## Dealing With Negative Reviews

Sooner or later, most authors will hear negative comments about their book or get a bad review. No matter how good your book is, there will always be people who find fault with it or simply don't like it. This is especially true for fiction, where reviews tend to be more subjective (especially reviews written by customers). Some people even make nasty remarks in reviews, or use reviews to further some agenda of their own. Don't take it personally or let it upset you. Even better, get motivated to get out there and solicit more good reviews.

On the other hand, it's important to study negative reviews and think about how you can improve your books. As writers, we need to be constantly learning and improving our craft. Of course, if the majority of reviews for a particular book are negative, then the book probably needs work.

Also keep in mind that most professional reviewers feel a responsibility to point out both the good and bad points of a book, in order to present a balanced view to the reader. Remember, the reviewer's responsibility is to serve their readers, not authors and publishers, and there's probably no such thing as a perfect book.

Many would argue that even a bad review is better than no review. There's an old saying that there's no such thing as bad publicity. With such a huge number of books competing for the attention of readers, any exposure could be helpful.

On online bookstores like Amazon, it can actually be helpful to have a few mediocre or even bad reviews because it makes the reviews look more genuine. When someone sees a book page with nothing but glowing 5-star reviews, they sometimes wonder if they were all written by the author's friends and family. And most shoppers probably realize that everyone has different tastes and a particular book simply won't appeal to all readers.

It's interesting to note that John Locke, the first independent author to sell more than one million books on Kindle, has a large number of negative reviews on the Amazon page for his book, *Saving Rachael*. Here's a summary of the reviews as of July 28, 2011:

## Potential Pitfalls With Book Reviews

| Customer Reviews | | |
|---|---|---|
| **447 Reviews** | | |
| 5 star: | (163) | **Average Customer Review** |
| 4 star: | (77) | ★★★☆☆ (447 customer reviews) |
| 3 star: | (42) | |
| 2 star: | (40) | |
| 1 star: | (125) | |

Clearly, bad reviews haven't stopped Locke from selling a vast number of books. But he also has numerous fans who buy all of the books in his Donovan Creed series. In fact, that's one of the major keys to his success – each time he releases a new book he has a large fan base that will buy it automatically. On Amazon, success breeds success, because the top selling books are highly visible to shoppers there.

Having said all of that, there are some steps that you can take if you get a review on an online bookstore that you feel is unjust or violates the site's policies. See Chapter 6 for more details about online bookstore reviews.

If you receive a review from another source that contains factual errors, or a plot spoiler, or that you believe is really unjustified, it's okay to contact the reviewer so long as you do so in a professional way. Write a polite letter to the reviewer, thanking them for the review, and pointing out the problem. You may be able to get the review changed, if it's online, or get a correction printed. But don't expect to change a reviewer's mind if they just didn't like the book.

Also consider the source of the review. Many online book reviews are written by people who are not professional book reviewers. Some of them simply don't know how to produce a properly written book review, or they allow their own personal biases and preferences to color their reviews.

*The Slippery Art of Book Reviewing*, by Mayra Calvani and Anne K. Edwards, describes instances where book bloggers have been harassed and even threatened by authors or publishers who are angry about reviews. If you do contact a reviewer about a negative review, keep your communication professional.

## Common Mistakes in Seeking Book Reviews

Here are some common mistakes in seeking book reviews:

- Failing to develop relationships with peers, book bloggers, and other influencers before asking for an endorsement or review. It's not always possible to do this, but it's certainly helpful. Leave constructive comments on their blogs and interact with them on social networks.

- Sending review copies too late. Plan your review schedule in advance and pay attention to the deadlines of the pre-publication reviewers.

- Not studying potential review outlets and their submission guidelines to determine if it's a good fit.

- Failing to understand the review process and different types of reviewers.

- Sending inadequate or unprofessional information to potential reviewers, and/or having no online presence. Some reviewers will want to know more about the book, author and/or publisher before making a decision whether to review a particular book. Make it easy for them to find what they need, and project a professional image.

- Being too pushy or presumptuous, or being too passive.

## 5
# Endorsements, Testimonials and Reviews

Don't underestimate the selling power of endorsements, testimonials and customer reviews. These reviews lend credibility by offering "social proof" that others value and recommend your book and they can make a real difference for customers who are on the fence about buying your book or comparing it to competing books. And don't forget that many people are influenced by celebrities and other high profile people.

*"Favorable comments help sell books because word-of-mouth is one of the most powerful forces in marketing! Anything you say about your book may appear self-serving and self-promotional, however words from high- profile people are not."*

Larry James
author of *How to Really Love the One You're With*

With today's information and entertainment overload, many book buyers rely on name recognition when buying products, including books. Consumers tend to buy books from authors they have heard of, which can make it difficult for new or little-known authors. The magic of endorsements is that the credibility of the high-profile endorser transfers to the author and the book being endorsed.

The terms "endorsement" and "testimonial" are often used interchangeably, but there is a difference. Endorsements are generally solicited from well-known people for promotional purposes. Testimonials are comments made by customers who purchased and read the book. A customer review is similar to a testimonial, but it's usually a little longer and focuses more on the content of the book, rather than just giving praise.

## Solicit Endorsements

Endorsements are recommendations from authors, experts or celebrities—people whose opinion can influence sales of your book. These are the quotes you typically see printed on the covers and inside of books and they are sometimes referred to as "blurbs."

Having a well-known person endorse your book lends credibility and can really impact sales, so it's worth the time and effort required to land important endorsements. But why would a high-profile individual do you the favor of giving you an endorsement? In a word: publicity. The person giving the endorsement gains exposure from endorsing quality products. And, of course, many people (especially other authors) are happy to help out an author who has written a good book.

Here are some steps for landing powerful endorsements:

1. **Schedule well in advance.**

    If you want to print your most important endorsements on your book cover or inside the book, you'll need to build time into your production schedule so you can get the text to your book designer in time. It can be time consuming to track down well-know people and get their endorsement, so start at least 60 to 90 days before you need the text.

## 2. Go for the gold!

The next step is to make a list of potential endorsers who are a good fit for the topic or genre of your book. Do not be afraid to aim high! You have nothing to lose but a little time and the cost of mailing a book. And the rewards of scoring an endorsement from a highly influential person can be great.

*"Your mission is to get the highest-placed, most influential opinion-molders in your field talking about your book. You have more control than you think over whom you quote, what they say and how you use their words."*

Dan Poynter, author of
*Dan Poynter's Self-Publishing Manual* and other books

It's best if endorsements come from people who are already known and respected by your target audience, but you can lend credibility to lesser known individuals through the credentials or book title after their name.

For nonfiction, seek out your own peers as well as top experts in your field, along with other high profile people who are a good fit for the book's topic. Your list might include:

- bestselling authors
- professors
- journalists
- politicians
- association leaders
- top bloggers
- prominent business leaders

Entertainers who have an interest in the topic you write about or whose fans match your target audience are also possible endorsers.

For fiction, seek endorsements from authors who write books similar to yours, both bestselling authors and lesser known authors. Also consider well-known people who are somehow related to the plot or characters in your story, are known to enjoy the type of book that you write, or whose fans match your target audience.

3. **Locate prospects.**

> It can be a challenge to track down an email or mailing address for top experts and celebrities. The first place to look is on the person's website. You might also try searching for their profile on Facebook, LinkedIn or Twitter. For authors, check their personal or author profile on Amazon.com and the publisher's website. You might also find contact information printed in the front or back of their books.
>
> Here are some resources for locating celebrities:
> http://ContactAnyCelebrity.com
> http://www.WhoRepresents.com
>
> *"If you're looking for actors, call the Screen Actors Guild (SAG) at 800-503-6737. Be prepared to stay on hold for a long time. Ask for the actor's agent or publicist. SAG is extremely busy and will give you only three contacts at a time."*
>
> Marilyn Ross and Sue Collier<br>authors of *The Complete Guide to Self-Publishing*
>
> If you know someone who knows someone important, you can ask them to make an initial contact on your

behalf. If you can't find contact information any other way, try contacting an agent or an author's publisher.

4. **Prepare your materials.**

If your book is not yet finished, prepare a synopsis, outline and a couple of sample chapters, along with a killer cover letter. If the manuscript is complete, you may still want to send a specific chapter that's relevant to the person you're asking for an endorsement, and offer to send the entire manuscript upon request.

It's a good idea to include some sample endorsements in the material you send. This is not as presumptuous as it might sound. Keep in mind that the people you are contacting are very busy and you are asking them for a favor. It takes some thought to write a good quotable endorsement and you can save the endorser's time by making a few suggestions. Spend time drafting two or three endorsements that fit each individual, and of course make it clear that these are only suggestions and they are welcome to modify or write something original.

Save time (yours and the prospects) by including the sample endorsements on a page that the endorser can sign and date to grant you permission to use their quote.

*"Ask them to talk about you in their quote rather than your book. For example, Jane Johnson is on a crusade to help all parents become exceptional parents. When you receive blurbs like that, you can use them to promote your talks, workshops and other products, in addition to using them on your book cover."*

Steve Harrison
Director of the Million Dollar Author Club

Be sure to edit and proofread the materials that you send out – you want to make the best possible impression. Prepare the materials before you start contacting prospects so that you can send them out immediately.

A good cover letter is concise, to the point, gracious, and humble. Start by introducing yourself and your book, mentioning any connection you have to the prospect, and explaining why you feel that the prospect is a good fit for the book. Then politely ask for an endorsement and thank them for their time. Include a deadline date of 30 to 45 days.

It's okay to let the prospect know about other high-profile endorsements that you have already received or are seeking. Success attracts success.

Do whatever you can to make it easy for the prospect to do you the favor of an endorsement. Provide all of your contact information (email, phone, fax, postal mail) and include a return envelope if you are sending a permission to quote through the mail.

5. **Consider Peer Reviews.**

    Peer reviews can be useful for getting feedback on your book and also generating endorsements. Nonfiction authors can send portions of their book to other experts in their field asking for professional feedback, and then send the completed manuscript later requesting an endorsement. Novelists can request peer reviews from top authors in their genre.

6. **Make contact.**

    The next step is to prioritize your list of potential endorsers and start making contact. You may have to go through assistants or agents, so be prepared to explain what you need.

*"The first thing you have to remember when you're trying to get a celebrity to endorse your book is that they'd be doing you a huge favor. Contact them in the way they wish to be contacted (mail, e-mail or fax) and follow their guidelines (or their agents' guidelines) to the letter."*

Penny C. Sansevieri
CEO, Author Marketing Experts

It is easiest to email a PDF document containing your manuscript or sample materials. You can combine your synopsis, outline and sample chapters or manuscript into one document, choose Save As in Word, and select PDF as the file type. If possible, consider offering Kindle or epub files of a completed book.

It's best to include a note offering to send hard copies if they prefer. Some people don't want to read on screen or print out a bunch of pages, and your job is to make it as easy as possible.

Also, consider sending your initial contact through the mail rather than email if you can locate an address. A physical package has more impact and it's harder to ignore than email. If you can't find a mailing address, try emailing the prospect first and asking for a mailing address so you can send the package.

7. **Follow up and confirm.**

If someone has not responded to your query or has promised an endorsement but hasn't delivered, you may need to follow up with a gentle reminder. If the prospect asks for a full manuscript or more information, send it immediately.

Once someone has given you an endorsement, be sure to get their written permission to use it. To protect yourself, get a signature and date on the endorsement. If the comments are given to you verbally, type it up (along with the celebrity name as they wish it to be listed) and send it with a space for date and signature and a request to fax or mail it back.

8. **Show your appreciation.**

Follow up promptly with a hand-written thank you note, and be sure to send the endorser an autographed copy of the book upon publication.

## Case Study – Get High-Profile Endorsements

Rabbi Ed Weinsberg secured an impressive number of endorsements from high profile individuals, including doctors and bestselling authors, for his book, *Conquer Prostate Cancer: How Medicine, Faith, Love and Sex Can Renew Your Life*. Here are some of the individuals who endorsed the book upon Rabbi Ed's request:

- John Gray, author of *Men Are from Mars, Women Are from Venus*

- Dr. Bernie Siegel, surgeon, cancer specialist, and author of *Faith, Hope and Healing: Inspiring Lessons Learned from People Living with Cancer*

- Rabbi Harold Kushner, author of *When Bad Things Happen to Good People*

- Dr. Ellen Kreidman, psychologist and expert in relationship and marriage enrichment in national media

- Stanley Smisskiss, founding chairman, American Cancer Society Foundation

- Kathy LaTour, editor, *Cure* magazine

- Rabbi Dov Peretz Elkins, co-editor of *Chicken Soup for the Jewish Soul*

- Dr. Edward Hallowell, author and psychiatrist specializing in anxiety disorders

- Peggy Huddleston, author of *Prepare for Surgery, Heal Faster: A Guide of Mind-Body Techniques*

- Dr. Vipul Patel, Director of Urological Oncology, Florida Hospital Cancer Institute

Here's what Rabbi Ed has to say about his experience in landing these endorsements:

"In seeking the endorsements of bestselling authors and experts, I sought out people who were opinion-molders in fields related to my book (cancer, faith, intimacy, and relationship-building). I was already acquainted on some level with six of the people on the above list and found it easy enough to simply phone them, but the other four initially didn't know me from Adam! So I made sure to introduce myself to the 'unknown greats' by sending an email asking if we could set up a time for a phone conversation about my new book. In some instances I got their attention by first developing some rapport with their gatekeepers.

I knew that my book would resonate with these people, given what I sensed about their kindred interests in my subject matter and my target audience of boomers and seniors. I pointed out the significance of the book's title and also gently reminded them of my credentials as a rabbi with a doctorate in gerontology. I figured they were more likely to regard me a peer because of my academic record and professional accomplishments.

I offered to send each of my prospective endorsers a few typed chapters of my book manuscript, unless they preferred the entire book. I also asked these individuals whether, out of consideration for their time, I should send them a brief sample of the kind of endorsement I was seeking. All but two said 'Yes!', but still consented to review my manuscript. I sent each person a different set of three to five sentences they might concur with, once they had read all or part of my manuscript. Along with the manuscript chapters, I added a title page and the table of contents, so they could see the book's entire scope. In some instances I sent the endorsement of other prominent people to persuade potential endorsers of my book's worth.

I was delighted that most of those who endorsed the book used some of the phrases I had suggested. They did so in part because my sample quotes were brief and to the point. More important, those who endorsed my book did so because they felt my topic was worthwhile, or because they enjoyed my upbeat writing style, or because they sensed that associating their names with my book would be good publicity for them. It helped that by the time I asked for an endorsement, I had honed my manuscript with repeated editing and I was confident that it would be recognized as top-notch."

## Seek a Foreword for Your Nonfiction Book

A foreword is a short introduction (around one to three pages) in the front of a book, usually written by a high-profile author or expert. A big name foreword can be even more powerful than an endorsement, in terms of lending credibility to the book. The foreword is usually mentioned on the bottom of the front cover and in promotional materials, for the publicity value. For example: Foreword by Jack Smith, author of *Important Book*.

You can approach a high-profile person in the same way as you would for an endorsement, but ask for a foreword instead. Or, ask someone who has already given you a glowing endorsement if they would be willing to write a foreword.

As with endorsements, it's helpful to write a draft or at least some ideas to save the person time. And be sure to spell "foreword" correctly – it is often misspelled as "forward."

The foreword is placed in the book after the table of contents and before the preface, acknowledgements and introduction (all of which are written by the book's author.)

## Savvy Tip

Consider offering to write endorsements or forewords for books that are being written by your peers. It's great publicity for you as well as for the book's author.

## Testimonials and Reader Reviews

Testimonials are similar to endorsements, but they are given by customers who liked a book so much that they were moved to share their praise. Testimonials typically consist of one to three sentences of praise such as, "I couldn't put this book down! It's a must-read for cozy mystery lovers."

Many testimonials are emailed to authors or posted on their websites. When someone makes a nice comment about your book, thank them and ask if you can use their quote in your marketing materials.

You may find that some customers become raving fans and are happy to share your book with others. It's important to show your appreciation to these folks and encourage them. For example, send your top fans a free autographed copy of your next book and ask for a testimonial and for them to help spread the word.

You can also solicit testimonials from your customers and clients by posting a message on your blog, newsletter or social networks. For example:

*"If you've read my book, Siren Song, I would really appreciate hearing what you thought of it."*

If you sell books directly to consumers, you can send a follow up email a week or two after purchase asking for feedback on the book. If your shopping cart has an autoresponder, this process is easily automated. Or you can send a broadcast email to a group of people asking if they could do you a favor and write a couple of lines about what they liked about the book and how it helped them.

Another approach is to offer a limited number of free copies of your book to your subscribers or network followers in exchange for testimonials or reviews. If you have a printed book, you could offer free ebook versions of the book to cut down on the cost.

## Case Study – Ask Loyal Followers to Review Your Book

A couple of weeks before this book was published, I posted a notice in my newsletter offering 20 free review copies of my book in exchange for a review. Hundreds of people responded to the offer and I drew 20 names from that list to send the review copies to upon publication.

I used my autoresponder service (Aweber) to handle the list signup and emails. I sent the book to 20 people from the list and sent a 20% off coupon to everyone else who responded. Here is the text that I posted in the newsletter:

**Get a Complimentary Copy of "How to Get Your Book Reviewed"**

Would you like a complimentary review copy of my new book, *How to Get Your Book Reviewed?* All I ask in return is an honest review of the book, posted on Amazon or BN.com. It doesn't need to be long - just a few sentences.

I am making available 20 review copies, in your choice of PDF, Kindle or epub format. Just sign up on this page and I'll draw 20 names from the list of everyone who signs up.

This is an exclusive offer for my subscribers, and the review copies will be available by the end of July. I'm really excited about this book and I look forward to sharing it with you!

Here's what the sign up page looked like:

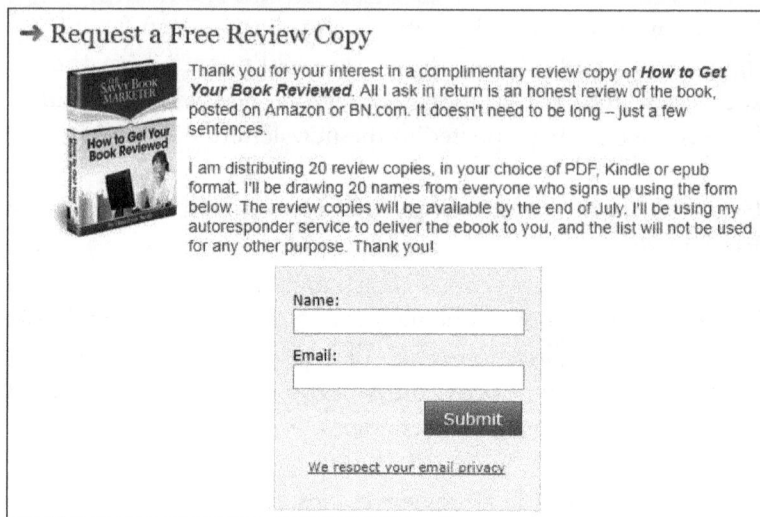

## Take Action

Never underestimate the power of endorsements, testimonials and customer reviews. Although it may be time consuming to pursue them, they can be worth their weight in gold in terms of generating sales. Map out a plan of action several months before publication and go for the gold!

In the next chapter, we will discuss how to get reviews and testimonials posted in online bookstores.

# 6

# Testimonials and Reviews in Online Bookstores

Online bookstores encourage customers to post testimonials and reviews to help others in choosing books. Testimonials are brief notes of praise for a book. Reader reviews tend to be a little longer than testimonials and focus more on the content of the book and on specifically what the reader liked or disliked about it. Not all reviews are positive.

Reader reviews are extremely important in the online selling environment. When consumers shop for books on online bookstores, many of them read the book reviews before they make a purchase. Even if they came to the site to buy a particular book, they may read the reviews to verify that they are making a good selection.

Positive reviews are a great selling point for all types of books, but they are especially important for nonfiction books, where consumers often compare several books on the same topic. Amazon actually encourages this, by displaying other similar books on your book's sales page.

In addition to influencing consumer behavior, reviews on Amazon can even influence how many customers see your book. The quantity and star ratings of a book's reviews appear to be one factor used in ranking books on the search results page when someone searches by keyword on Amazon.

Don't forget to monitor your online reviews. Stop by your book sales page on each bookstore periodically to check out your new reviews, and share the best reviews with others through your social networks. If the review was posted by someone you know, be sure to send them a thank you note.

## Case Study – Do Reviews Really Influence Book Purchases?

The Yale School of Management studied customer reviews at Amazon.com and BN.com and produced a report titled "The Effect of Word of Mouth on Sales: Online Book Reviews." Below is an excerpt from the report, which can be viewed at http://www.weberbooks.com/reviews.pdf.

"Since Amazon has many more reviewers than rivals, its reviews are on average quite lengthy, and its reviews are on average quite positive, it seems plausible to at least speculate that the total number of books sold at Amazon is higher than it would have been absent the provision of customer review features. Further, and more interestingly, our results show that customers certainly behave as if the fit between customer and book is improved by using reviews to screen purchases. This evidence suggests that customer word-of-mouth has a causal impact on consumer purchasing behavior . . ."

Reading between the academic-speak, it seems that the researchers believe that reviews not only influence sales of individual books, but they increase overall sales on Amazon.com (something that Amazon is quite well aware of!).

## Actively Solicit Reviews on Online Bookstores

So, what's the secret to getting reviews on online bookstores (besides writing a great book)? ASK people to post reviews and make it EASY for them by providing a link to your book page or directly to the review screen.

Here are some ideas for inviting people to post reviews on online bookstores:

- When you send out review copies to colleagues and influencers seeking endorsements, ask them if they will also post the testimonial or a brief review on Amazon or Barnes & Noble. If you have sent manuscripts before the book was published, follow up after publication asking if they would be kind enough to post their comments on one of these sites.

- Any time someone writes a positive review of your book, ask them to post it on Amazon or Barnes & Noble. Before contacting the reviewer, check to see if they have already posted the review, because many reviewers do that routinely.

- Make an occasional post on your social networks, blog or newsletter, asking people to post a review on Amazon or BN.com if they enjoyed your book. Be sure to include a link to your book review page on one or both sites.

- When you receive an email or other correspondence praising your book, reply with a thank you note and a request to post a book review on Amazon or Barnes & Noble. If someone has taken the time to write to you about your book, they are obviously a fan and will probably be happy to post a book review for you. Here's a sample message:

> *Thanks so much for your note. I love getting feedback from readers and I'm glad that you enjoyed the book.*
>
> *I would really appreciate your taking a few minutes to post your comments or a brief review on my Amazon page at www.example.com. Look for the "customer reviews" section about halfway down the page and click on the "create your own review" button to the right. Or, use this link to go directly to the review form: http://shortlink.com.*
>
> *If you're a Barnes & Noble customer, click the "write a review" button at www.bn.com/mybookpage.*
>
> *Reviews are helpful to shoppers and can make a big difference in book sales, and I would be grateful for your help.*

When you email your fans, also ask for permission to use a portion of the customer's message to you as a testimonial quote on your own website. In your request, I suggest pulling out the portion you want to use and formatting it as a quote so the customer can see exactly what it will look like.

- Another way to find potential reviewers is to contact people who are active in forums and discussion boards that are relevant to the topic of your book.

- You can ask family members and friends to post a review (or they may offer to do so), but be very careful. Anyone who shares your last name will look like a relative. Also, you don't want the reviews to sound contrived. For example, posting something like "My friend Susan has written a great book and everyone should read it" is not a good idea. And of course you want these folks to post an honest opinion—you might ask them to write a few sentences stating what they liked best about the book.

- It's not a good idea to write a review of your own book. Doing so may turn people off or cause them to question the validity of your other reviews. Amazon doesn't allow authors to review their own books, and if someone reports you the review will be removed.

## Savvy Tip

You can create a link directly to the book review form by clicking on the "create your own review" button and then using a URL shortening service to create a short link to the form. To save time, save your review request email in a Word document and copy and paste it as needed.

## Case Study – Getting Reviews on Amazon

Tony Eldridge's first self-published novel, *The Samson Effect,* has 33 reviews on Amazon, almost all 5-star. Here's what he has to say about Amazon reviews:

"One thing I'm proud of is that most of the reviews on *The Samson Effect* came from people I didn't know. I tended not to ask my relatives to review the book because I didn't want one to say, 'My son's book is the greatest ever written!' – Signed, Tony's Mother.

That said, any time someone took the time to email me or tell me in person how much they liked the book, I always, always, always asked them if they would mind writing a review on Amazon. Conversely, if people gave me suggestions on how to make the book better, I thanked them, but I never asked them to do a review.

The reviews came slowly, over four years, but they came. To this day, I think that reviews do play a big role in sales. I believe they can be a tipping point when people are trying to decide what books to read next. I know they are with me."

## Reviews on Amazon.com

Amazon is by far the largest online bookseller and the most important place for your reviews to appear. Anyone who has an Amazon user name and password and has purchased any product on Amazon.com can review your book there, even if they purchased your book elsewhere or got a free review copy.

To post a review, look for the Customer Reviews section about halfway down the page and click on the Create Your Own Review button. Reviews can be done in written or video format, and it may take up to 48 hours for them to appear on the site after they are posted.

Also note that Amazon does not accept reviews for books until the publication date listed in the Amazon database, so you cannot write reviews there prior to publication.

Here's what a review looks like on Amazon:

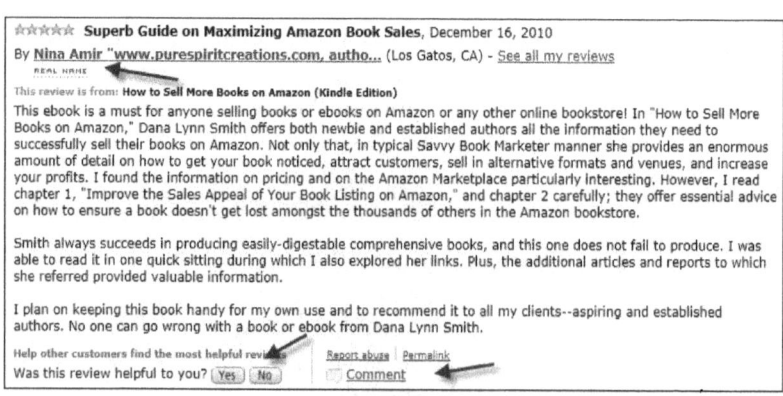

The star rating and review headline appear at the top of the review. Below that is the name and "signature" of the reviewer. Below the review is a button that people can click to "vote" on the review by indicating if they found it helpful. Be sure to click **Yes** on your good reviews. Next to that are three more links.

The **Report Abuse** link lets you report violations of Amazon's review policy. When you click on that link you will see this message:

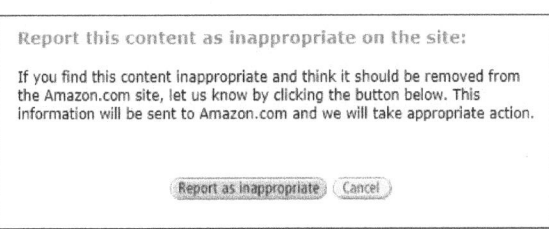

If you really disagree with what someone wrote in a review on Amazon, you can click the **Comment** button and write a note, but be careful not to sound defensive or attack the reviewer. Keep it polite and professional.

If a review gets enough negative votes and comments, it may be removed.

You can read the current version of Amazon's review guidelines at http://amzn.to/kgi5L6.

It's interesting to note that Amazon requires reviewers who receive a free review copy to disclose that fact, although many reviewers do not (and are probably not even aware of the rule).

Here are some of the things that Amazon does NOT allow in reviews:

- Crucial plot elements (unless you include a clear "spoiler alert")
- Links to the reviewer's own books.
- Advertisements, promotional material or repeated posts that make the same point excessively

- Sentiments by or on behalf of a person or company with a financial interest in the product or a directly competing product (including reviews by authors)
- Reviews written for any form of compensation other than a free copy of the product
- Solicitations for helpful votes
- Phone numbers, postal mailing addresses, and URLs external to Amazon.com

## Seek Reviews on Amazon

Sending review copies to people who have already reviewed books like yours on Amazon can be a terrific way to get more reviews posted on Amazon. There are two ways to find potential reviewers, and both will take an investment of time.

1. Scroll down the list of Amazon's top reviewers, looking for people who seem to be a good fit for your book.

2. Search for books similar to yours on Amazon and then scroll through the reviewers looking for good candidates.

You can use one or both of these strategies. Below I'll discuss both methods and offer some tips for choosing the best candidates and making contact.

## Top Amazon Reviewers

The most prolific reviewers have posted thousands of product reviews on Amazon.com. These top reviewers are ranked by Amazon based on several criteria, including the number of reviews and the number of positive votes on those reviews.

When these top reviewers post a review on Amazon, it's designated with a "badge" that says something like "Top 500

Reviewer" or "Top 100 Reviewer." You will see the badge just beneath the reviewer's name on their Amazon reviews. Here's an example:

> ★★★★★ **All-new material from the funniest man in America**, May 12, 2010
> By <u>Julie Neal</u> (Sanibel Island, Fla.) - <u>See all my reviews</u>
> TOP 100 REVIEWER    VINE™ VOICE    REAL NAME

Having a review from one of these top reviewers lends extra credibility to your book. Many of these people also post their reviews on other websites, so you are likely to get additional exposure from their reviews. They may also post a number of **ListMania** lists and **So You'd Like To** guides on Amazon, giving products further exposure.

You can search the list of the top 1,000 Amazon reviewers at http://www.amazon.com/review/top-reviewers.

Ten people are listed per page. Hover your mouse over a reviewer's name to see a brief overview, including what their interests are. Click on the name to see their full Amazon profile, or click the list of reviews beneath their name to see their reviews. Remember, people can review any product sold on Amazon, not just books, so it will probably take some digging to find appropriate reviewers. The top reviewers probably receive numerous requests for reviews, so don't be surprised if they are not open to solicitations.

## Amazon Vine Reviewers

In the screenshot above, notice the "Vine Voice" badge next to "Top 100 Reviewer." This indicates that the reviewer is also part of the elite Amazon Vine™ review program. These top reviewers are invited by Amazon to join the Vine program and receive a newsletter listing new books and other products provided by publishers and manufacturers for review on Amazon.

There appears to be no way for self-publishers to submit books to the Vine program, but you can still contact these reviewers directly. It's a safe bet that these reviewers are influential and most of them are probably on the Top Reviewers list, but you still need to make sure that they are a good fit for your book before making contact.

## Research Reviewers of Books Similar to Yours

My preferred method is to skim over the reviews of other books that are similar to yours (or reach your same target audience) and look for reviewers who are a good fit. If those people also have a Top Reviewer badge, all the better.

You can find books to research in several ways:

- Select **Books** from the drop down menu near the top of the page on Amazon.com and then enter keywords in the search box.

- Browse for books in your genre or topic area:
    - Go to Amazon.com
    - Click on **Books** in the menu on the left side of the screen.
    - Choose your category or genre from the list on the left, then choose sub-categories as necessary.

- Look for the bestselling books in your genre or topic area:
    - Go to Amazon.com
    - Click on **Books** in the menu on the left side of the screen.
    - Click the Bestsellers button in the main menu bar near the top.

- Choose your category or genre from the list on the left, then choose sub-categories as necessary.

You can also repeat the last two steps above, selecting **Kindle** instead of **Books** from the left menu. That will allow you to find books that are published only in Kindle format.

When searching or browsing by category, don't be surprised to find that a lot of books are classified in the wrong category.

Once you have located books of interest, scroll down to the reviews section and skim over the positive reviews looking for reviewers who would be a good fit for your book.

## Select the Best Potential Reviewers and Find Contact Information

Read some of the person's reviews to see if you like their style. Some reviewers write balanced reviews, while others tend to be harsh in their criticism. On Amazon, you can learn more about a reviewer by clicking on their name to see their personal profile. On the left side of the profile look for the **In My Own Words** and **Interests** sections to learn more about the reviewer. Many reviewers will list the type of books that they like to read and they may also indicate whether or not they accept review requests and how they prefer to be contacted.

Some reviewers list their email address, social networks, or website address on their profile. Previously there was a button on the profile to connect with people through the Amazon friends feature, but as of this writing that feature is gone. You may also be able to find contact information by searching online for the reviewer's blog or website.

## Update Your Amazon Profile

Before you start contacting reviewers, it's a good idea to update your own profile on Amazon. If you have purchased anything on Amazon.com, you already have a profile. To update your profile, follow these steps:

- Log into your Amazon account.
- Click on **YOURNAME's Amazon Account** near the top of the screen.

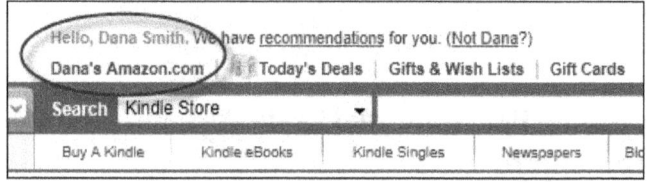

- Click on **Your Profile** from the menu bar near the top.
- Click on the yellow **Edit Your Profile** button near the top right.
- Enter your tagline in the **Signature** field to the left. Be brief – only about 25 characters will be visible on your reviews. Examples: "romantic suspense author" or "The Savvy Book Marketer"
- Update other information as necessary, including writing a brief bio or description in the **In My Own Words** field. Also upload your author photo.
- Click on **Save Your Profile** in the upper right.

## Contact Potential Reviewers on Amazon

Once you have made a list of potential reviewers, send them an email inviting them to review your book. The email should include the book title, genre, and a strong synopsis. You can also include a link to your book's page on Amazon and a link to your website's media room. You might also offer to email them the first chapter of the book so they can get a taste of it. Also ask if they prefer to review printed books or Kindle books.

*"If you spend two or three days contacting about 300 potential Amazon reviewers, you can expect to receive about 40 to 50 responses, and wind up with perhaps 35 reviews, a quite satisfactory result."*

Steve Weber
author of *Plug Your Book! Online Book Marketing for Authors*

## Reviews by Amazon Editors

Amazon actually posts some book reviews and recommendations from their own staff. This is a long shot, but the reward could be great. It's possible that books submitted may be considered for the Amazon Vine program as well. Here are the instructions from the Amazon site:

"Our editorial team organizes feature presentations, and you're welcome to send them promotional materials or review copies. To submit your book for possible feature or review, send it via the U.S. Postal Service to the address below. Please refer to our extensive list of subject areas to determine which category would best represent your book. Indicating a category will ensure that your request is processed in the most efficient manner possible.

Amazon.com
Attn: Editorial - [Product & Category]
701 Fifth Avenue
Suite 1500
Seattle WA 98104

Once your materials are received, they'll be passed along to the appropriate editor(s). Please know that we receive many editorial submissions each week, and we are unable to acknowledge receipt of a review copy, nor are we able to speculate on whether or not we will be able to review or otherwise promote your title."

## Amazon Links

Amazon review guidelines: http://amzn.to/kgi5L6

Amazon's discussion forum for discussing book reviews: http://bit.ly/mQ2maG

Amazon's Publisher FAQ page: http://amzn.to/rlnC8P

## Reviews on BarnesAndNoble.com

Barnes & Noble (BN.com) is the second largest online seller of books in the U.S. (They are a rather distant second in online print sales, although they are gaining some ground on Amazon in ebook sales.)

The BN.com review policies are located at http://bit.ly/kconRo

B&N's policies are similar to Amazon's, but there are a few differences.

For example, Amazon asks reviewers to clearly label their reviews as having plot spoilers (something that gives away too much of the story or the ending in a novel), but Barnes & Noble will actually remove a review that contains a spoiler.

B&N's list of prohibited items in reviews includes:

- HTML tags
- Profanity, obscenities, or vulgarities
- Comments that defame anyone

- Time-sensitive information such as tour dates, signings, lectures, etc.
- Single-word reviews. Other people will read your review to discover why you liked or didn't like the title. Be descriptive.
- Comments focusing on the author
- Comments that may ruin the ending for others
- Phone numbers, addresses, URLs
- Pricing and availability information or alternative ordering information
- Advertisements or commercial solicitation

Use the Report this Review button to report violations of B&N's review policies. You will see a pop-up box like this:

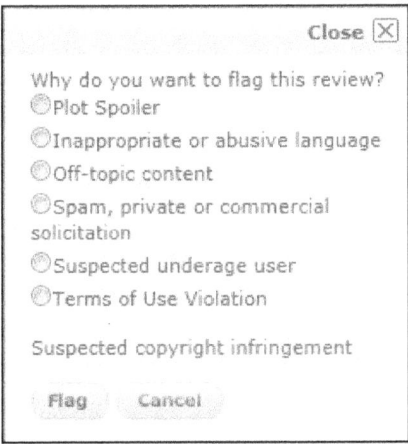

Like Amazon, BN.com requires reviewers to have an account on the site and to have purchased something there. While most readers have an account on Amazon.com, many people do not have an account on BN.com, so the pool of people who can post reviews there is smaller.

## Other Online Bookstores

Several other online bookstores, such as Powells.com and Booksamillion.com allow the posting of book reviews, but generally you have to have an account on the site to post reviews. Given the relatively small amount of traffic on these sites it may not be a good investment of your time to pursue reviews there.

# 7

# Virtual Reader Communities

Virtual reader communities are a specialized type of social networking site where readers and authors network, and readers recommend books to others. I think they are most effective for novelists, but they can also be useful for nonfiction and children's authors.

Similar to other social networks, you join the site, set up a profile, and start making friends. The difference here is that you are talking about books you have read, are currently reading, or want to read. You can add books to your list, rate and review them, discuss books with others, and sign up to follow your favorite authors.

Many of these sites provide a way for authors to communicate with fans and promote their books. The key is to participate and not just show up to promote your books. It's also important to read the rules on each site to see what authors are and are not allowed to do.

You can get reviews on these sites by asking peers and customers who give you testimonial quotes and reviews if they will post reviews for you.

## Savvy Tip

Doing a free book giveaway on a virtual reader community is a great way to get reviews posted on these important online reader communities. Winners of these giveaways are encouraged, but not required, to post a review on the site.

## Goodreads

Goodreads at http://www.goodreads.com/author/program is the largest virtual reader community (with 1.8 million users) and I recommend joining and becoming active. You will need to be logged into your Goodreads account to access some of the Goodreads links in this section.

I suggest using the **Goodreads Giveaway** promotion as part of your book launch (but you can also do it at a later date.) You choose how many copies you want to give away and the dates for the promotion. Members enter to win a free copy of your book. At the end of the contest, Goodreads draws the winners and sends you their addresses so you can ship the books.

Goodreads encourages the winners to write a review of the book. You can enclose a cover letter with the book politely requesting a review. Even if you don't get any reviews, you get good publicity on the site.

Join Goodreads: http://www.goodreads.com/author/program.

Details of book giveaway program:
http://www.goodreads.com/giveaway/new

Tips on using Goodreads: http://bit.ly/dsE3bJ

To find popular books similar to yours, select your genre from the list on this page: http://www.goodreads.com/book

## LibraryThing

LibraryThing is similar to Goodreads and has more than 1.3 million members. Registered authors can promote events, participate in Author Chat, and do a book giveaway.

Author pages are automatically generated on LibraryThing as soon as someone adds one of their books to a library. Anyone can add information, photos, and links to the author's page, although authors have the option of not allowing comments on their pages.

To become an official LibraryThing Author, you must be a member of LibraryThing who is also a published (or about-to-be-published) author, and your book(s) must be entered into LibraryThing.

Author opportunities on LibraryThing:
http://www.librarything.com/about_authors.php

## Other Virtual Reader Communities

Here are several other major virtual reader communities to consider joining if time permits:

### weRead

weRead is an online community for book lovers where members can rate and review books and network with other readers. Authors can register at this page:
http://weread.com/register.php?authorRegistration=true

### Authors Den
Authors can build profile pages on AuthorsDen and interact with others on AuthorsDen, review books, and bookmark and share their stories, articles, and blogs. See sample author profiles at:

http://www.authorsden.com/visit/author.asp?AuthorID=87673

## Shelfari

Shelfari is a gathering place for authors, aspiring authors, publishers, and readers where users build virtual bookshelves, share recommendations, participate in book groups, and influence the community by rating and discussing books.

Shelfari also offers a bookshelf application for Facebook, which allows you to build a bookshelf on your profile showcasing your favorite books (including your own, of course), then rate and review what you've read. You can also connect with readers who share your interests. Shelfari was launched in late 2006 and acquired by Amazon in August 2008.

Join at: http://www.shelfari.com

## Red Room

Red Room requires authors to apply for author status and be approved. Join the site first as a reader and start participating, then register for author status. Apply to Red Room at:

Join at http://www.redroom.com/become-red-room-author.

## Nothing Binding

This social networking site for authors and readers is geared toward independent publishers.

Nothing Binding allows authors to promote their books, connect with other authors and book buyers, and discover great new books. The site was created by publishing industry veteran Jerry D. Simmons. Join at: http://www.nothingbinding.com

## JacketFlap

JacketFlap is a social networking community that focuses on children's and young adult books. Members are a diverse group of more than 3,800 published authors and illustrators as well as teachers, librarians, parents, students, publishers, aspiring authors, and others.

JacketFlap also boasts the world's largest database of information about children's book publishers, with listings for 32,000 publishers of all sizes. Included are submission guidelines for thousands of the publishers in the system.

Join at: http://www.jacketflap.com

## WorldCat

WorldCat at: http://www.worldcat.org is an online catalog of library book collections.

The site, designed as a tool to facilitate inter-library lending, catalogs the collections of more than 10,000 libraries worldwide. If your local library doesn't have a book that you want, they can borrow it from another library.

WorldCat has also added some social features to their site. Users can create lists of books, write book reviews, and assign keyword tags to books. You can add keyword tags to your book to make it easier for others to find. Reader reviews from Amazon.com appear on the review page, but you can enter other reviews on that page, or invite someone to write a review there.

WorldCat is a great tool for estimating how many libraries have purchased your book, and you can see specifically which libraries have the book. Just enter your book title in the search field to get a list of participating libraries that have the book.

The results page is arranged by physical location, sorting the results by the libraries nearest to you. If you have a lot of listings, you may need to enter different states in the "enter location information" field in order to see all of your listings.

Because not all libraries participate in the WorldCat database, the information on your library book sales will not be complete. Approximately 60 to 75 percent of U.S. public libraries participate and it varies by state, with all libraries in some states participating.

**IndieBound**

IndieBound helps shoppers connect with independent bookstores.

On the site users can create a book wish list that can be sent to family and friends, create profile pages and build a network of online friends, and join the affiliate program to sell books from their own website.

Learn more at http://www.indiebound.org/indie-community.

Below are some other reader communities to consider:

- 1 Chapter Free http://www.1chapterfree.com

- All Fiction Books http://www.allfictionbooks.com

- Best Books Reviewed http://www.bestbooksreviewed.com

- Bibliophil www.bibliophil.org

- Book Hitch http://www.bookhitch.com

## Virtual Reader Communities

- Book Reporter http://www.bookreporter.com

- Book Teaser's Galore
  http://bookteasersgalore.blogspot.com

- Books for Women by Women
  http://www.booksbywomenforwomen.com

- Internet Book Database http://www.ibookdb.net

- Once Written http://www.oncewritten.com

- Overbooked http://www.overbooked.org (fiction)

- Reader 2 http://reader2.com

How to Get Your Book Reviewed

# 8

# Book Review Blogs

Thousands of blogs and websites regularly post reviews of books. Book review websites may review a lot of books and have multiple reviewers. Book blogs are typically written by a single person (who may also be an author) in a blog format and may contain other content in addition to the book reviews. For the sake of convenience, we will refer to all of these sites as book blogs.

Book bloggers usually post reviews on their own site and on Amazon.com, and sometimes on other sites as well. Many blogs devoted to book reviews also post interviews with authors or sponsor book giveaways or contests.

Most book review blogs focus on fiction, often in a particular genre, although some review nonfiction as well. Top bloggers in categories such as romance, fantasy, and mystery can be strong opinion makers and really influence sales, as you will see in the following case study.

## Case Study – The Amanda Hocking Story

If you doubt the power of book blogs, consider Amanda Hocking's story. In March of 2010, after several years of writing books and being rejected by publishers, then 25-year-old Hocking published her first novel in paperback format through Lulu and in ebook format on the Kindle store. She published two more books soon afterward.

In a blog post at http://bit.ly/oqNRXE, she describes how her discovery of book bloggers skyrocketed her sales from 624 books in May to 4,258 in June.

After quitting her day job and focusing on writing and publishing full time, Hocking's sales grew at an incredible rate over the next six months. *USA Today* reported that Hocking sold 450,000 copies of her nine books in January of 2011, and 99% of those sales were ebooks. In March of 2011, Hocking signed a four-book publishing deal with St. Martin's Press, reportedly worth more than $2 million.

## Working With Book Blogs

It's helpful to have an understanding of the blogger's perspective. Here are some points to consider:

- Most book blogs are run by individuals like you and me. The blogger may be an author or editor, or just someone who loves good books and wants to share them with others.

- Some of the larger book blogs have a group of volunteer reviewers, but many are operated by a single person.

- Bloggers have other demands on their time—such as a job, family, and other projects—so reading, writing reviews, and maintaining a website must be done in their "spare" time.

- Many bloggers have large piles of books to process, some of which aren't even appropriate for their blog because the author or publisher failed to read the submission guidelines. They may also get a large number of email queries. It's quite time consuming to process all those books and emails.

- If a blogger agrees to review your book, it may take months for the review to appear due to the backlog of books already ahead of yours.

- Most book blogs are primarily labors of love. Typically the blogger or reviewer's only compensation is the books they receive. Some of the most popular blogs earn income from advertising or Amazon commissions, but in most cases it's not much income. And blog owners have to pay for web hosting fees and any necessary technical assistance out of their own pocket.

- Reviewing books can be a fairly thankless job, and outstanding bloggers may not get the recognition they deserve.

With those points in mind, here are some tips for working successfully with book bloggers:

- Always be polite and appreciative of the work that book bloggers do.

- Get to know bloggers first by leaving comments on their site and networking on sites like Goodreads,

Facebook, Twitter and the Book Blogs social network on Ning at http://bookblogs.ning.com.

- Study each site and read the submission guidelines to determine if your book is a good fit for the site. If there are no guidelines posted and you aren't quite sure, send an email inquiry. You will find that some book blogs have no contact information or link listed, probably because they don't wish to receive email.

- Send a personalized email or cover letter to selected bloggers. You can save time by writing a template in advance, but be sure to personalize the first paragraph with a mention of their site.

- Make sure your email or cover letter is concise, engaging, and gracious. Ask how you can be of help to them.

- See chapter 3 for more guidelines on what to send to book bloggers. It's also a good idea to email your cover artwork to a blogger who has agreed to a review, or send a link to the page on your website where they can download the cover.

- Think beyond reviews. Bloggers who are inundated with books to review may appreciate the offer of an author interview (written, audio, or video), a book giveaway, a free chapter download, a guest post about the craft of writing, or something else fun to offer their readers.

- After sending the book, follow up with an email in about two to four weeks. It's less pushy to inquire if the book was received, rather than asking when they are going to post a review. Include a one or two sentence summary of the book's contents, to jog their memory about your book. Remember that the reviewer probably has a big pile of books to read, and it may take months to get to yours. But a gentle reminder from you might cause them to pull your book from the pile for another look.

As we will discuss in the next chapter, some book review blogs offer an express review service, where they will do a review within a certain time frame in return for a payment. Most blogs that offer this service also do free reviews of appropriate books, as they can get to them.

## Finding Book Blogs

The next step is to find book blogs that are a good fit for your book and offer you the best possible audience. Here are some ways to find potential review sites:

- Use a search engine like Google to search for book blogs and book review sites. Novelists should search first for sites specific to their genre, using terms such as "book blog romance," "science fiction book reviews," and "book blog + fantasy." Then expand your search to more general book review sites.

- Look at the website of books similar to yours and see if they have reviews from any relevant sites.

- Ask other authors in your book genre or topic for recommendations.

- Check the blogroll or links section of each blog that you visit for links to similar sites.

You may also want to join social networks for book bloggers, such as Book Blogs at http://bookblogs.ning.com.

- Read the rules at: http://bit.ly/oVZySY

- Post book giveaways at: http://bookblogs.ning.com/group/bookbloggiveaways

- Promote books at: http://bookblogs.ning.com/group/promoteyourbooks

Below are links to several free lists of book bloggers available online. Some of these lists are more up to date than others, but they make a good starting point for research.

- Indie Book Reviewer Guide – blogs that review self-published books. Scroll to the bottom for some Kindle only reviewers and also links to some other lists of reviewers.
  http://www.stepbystepselfpublishing.net/reviewer-list.html

- The Indie Review – list of blogs that accept independently published books and ebooks.
  http://www.theindieview.com (subscribe to get the list)

- Review Sites from Angela Wilson at Market My Novel
  http://marketmynovel.com (look in the right column of this site for reviewers)

- Review Sites from Karina Fabian
  http://bit.ly/pK4SqZ (scroll down the page)

- Review Sites from Robin Mizzel
  http://robinmizell.wordpress.com/book-reviewers/

## Researching Book Blogs

Once you have a list of possible candidates, it's important to research each one to determine if it's a good fit. Here are some research tips:

- Read the submission requirements to make sure your book meets the blog's guidelines and also find out whether you should send an email query, send an ebook, or mail a printed book.

- If your book is only available in ebook format, make sure the review site reviews ebooks.

- If your book is self-published, try to determine whether the site accepts self-published books. Some review sites specifically state this, but many do not. If there's no mention and you think the book is a good fit, consider submitting it.

- Sometimes it's a challenge to find the submissions page or contact information. Look in the menu across the top, scroll down the sidebar, and look for links at the very bottom of the page.

- Review sites that do not have submissions or contact information probably do not accept unsolicited books, preferring to just review whatever books the reviewer is reading.

- Consider how many reviews are posted on the site and how often reviews are posted. Sites that post a lot of reviews may have more than one reviewer, which may increase the chances of your book being selected for review.

- Try to estimate the amount of traffic (number of visitors) that the site receives. More details on this are included in the next section.

- Read a few reviews of books similar to yours and study the reviewer's style. Some reviews are well written, thoughtful commentaries on the book, while others are little more than a repeat of the book's promotional copy. Some reviewers only review books they really like, while others write quite critical reviews of some books.

Yes, it takes a lot of time to do the research, but you'll be wasting time and money if you send review copies to bloggers who aren't interested in the type of books you write.

## Estimating the Number of Blog Visitors

Ideally, you want your reviews to appear on sites that are the best fit for your book and your target audience, and have the highest number of visitors.

Getting a review on a popular blog can generate a lot of interest in your book, but don't completely ignore lower traffic sites. There may be less competition for getting reviews on these sites, and they can still generate reviews on Amazon, provide backlinks to your website, and generate good review quotes for marketing purposes.

One of the easiest ways to estimate the relative traffic of one site vs. another one is to check the site's Alexa rank. Copy the website's URL into the search box at http://www.alexa.com/siteinfo.

When you click the Search button, you'll get both a worldwide rank and a ranking for the country where the site is located.

These rankings change constantly. Here's an example for my own website:

The lower the ranking, the more estimated traffic the site gets. The top site, Google, is ranked #1. Having a lot of incoming links from other websites is also a positive sign. Just as a point of reference, my site ranks about 112,007 worldwide and 26,406 in the U.S. and it has about 250 unique visitors a day.

Keep in mind that Alexa rankings are not very accurate for sites with low traffic. But they can help you estimate the relative traffic of one site vs. another one. A site with a ranking of 100,000 should get a lot more traffic than a site with a ranking of 1,000,000.

Another indication of the popularity of a book blog is the number of comments on the site. If you see lots of comments on the reviews, the site probably has an active, engaged audience.

## Virtual Book Tours

On a virtual book tour, authors visit a series of blogs, radio shows, or other virtual venues during a certain time frame – usually one to three weeks – to promote their book. Most tour stops involve making guest posts on blogs (either by writing an article or being interviewed by the blog owner) or having the blogger review the book.

When planning your tour, look for book blogs related to your book's topic or genre, general book blogs, and blogs that cater to the specific target audience for your book.

Organizing a virtual book tour is a lot of work, so be sure to start early. Here are the basic steps to planning a tour:

- Decide on the tour dates.
- Identify blogs and other potential tour hosts that are a good fit for your book.
- Write a good letter of invitation that outlines the benefit to the host.
- Set up a schedule for the tour.
- Send review copies of your book to the hosts.
- Correspond with the hosts and follow up as necessary.
- Write an article or interview for each tour stop (unless the host is reviewing the book or interviewing you.)
- Set up a tour page on your website to list the schedule and links to tour stops.
- Promote the tour in partnership with the hosts.
- Visit the host's website on the day of the tour stop and for about a week afterward to respond to comments.
- Send a thank you note to each host.

There are several blog tour organizers that can handle many of the details for you and coordinate with the hosts. Their fees reflect the amount of time that goes into tour coordination as well as their contacts with potential tour hosts.

For detailed information on planning a virtual book tour, see my how-to guide at www.VirtualBookTourMagic.com.

## Case Study – Do Virtual Book Tours Work?

*Children's book author Fiona Ingram shares her experience with virtual book tours in this article, reprinted with permission.*

Do blog tours work? In my experience the answer is a resounding yes. My tour literally propelled my author profile into the stratosphere and I still get Google Alerts from it. Here are some reasons why I think blog tours are effective:

- Massive exposure to an audience you possibly would never have found on your own. Each blog stop has its own followers. There are also people who enjoy following the complete tour, so blogs get new readers, and you, the guest, get a whole lot of attention.

- You are invited to write posts about yourself, your work, your book, and your writing techniques that give more interesting angles to you as an author. I felt challenged in a positive sense because many of my blog hosts asked me for posts relating to kids' literacy, making reading more interesting for kids, how to get kids back into books, how to write for kids. It was great!

- Within a short space of time those blog posts start appearing on other people's blog pages, pop up in Google Alerts, and there is a general spread of awareness as more and more people either follow the blog tour post by post, or simply pass on the information they have found through their own feeds. This can also be through emails, Twitter, Facebook and other social sites. When people enjoy something, they comment on it.

- Book giveaways are a wonderful way of getting people to comment and participate in the tour. Your blog tour hosts usually arrange this; you have to get the books to the hosts first.

- If people enjoy reading about you they may ask the blog tour organizers to add you to their blog as a guest post. I gained a few more stops on my tour once people began reading my posts.

What you can do to maximize your success:

- Send a personal email to all your blog hosts in advance thanking them for the opportunity to appear on their blog, and confirming date, time, their blog address, topic of the post, and when they can expect the information. Make sure they receive your post well in advance.

- Have a look at each blog on your tour and get a feel for the tone of it. Is it intellectual, chatty, quirky, fun, formal, etc? Tailor your post to reflect the tone of the blog.

- If you are sending a giveaway or review copies of your book, make sure this is done well in advance and confirm with your blog tour organizers that the hosts have received their copies.

- Make sure you visit each blog stop for a few days afterwards to reply to comments. Your blog tour organizers will usually get the ball rolling by commenting first. Make it easy for yourself by setting an email request for when comments are made on the various posts. This will help you stay in touch.

Blog tours are a great way to develop new readers, fans, and friends, and to meet people interested in your work.

*Fiona Ingram is the author of a children's middle-grade adventure novel* **The Secret of the Sacred Scarab** *at* *http://www.secretofthesacredscarab.com.*

*Her blog is at http://fionaingramauthor.blogspot.com.*

# 9
# Paid Book Reviews

Several companies offer paid book review services. In addition, some online book review sites that do free reviews also offer express review services, providing a review within a certain time frame in exchange for payment.

The practice of paying for book reviews is very controversial. Some people think that paid book reviews are by nature biased because they are done for a fee, that they have no credibility with readers, or that it's a waste of money because there are so many other avenues for getting book reviews.

*"Take what you would have spent getting a paid review and use it to send free books to avid readers. Real enthusiasm from a reader is worth more than any paid review. You can then ask those readers for permission to use their comments in your promotional materials."*

M.J. Rose
Bestselling author of 11 novels,
co-author with Angela Adair Hoy of *How to Publish and Promote Online,* and co-author with Doug Clegg of *Buzz Your Book*

Others maintain that paid reviews can be just as fair and professional as other reviews, and that reviewers deserve to be compensated for their time. They argue that only a fraction of new books can be covered in the traditional review journals each year, and that self-published books are discriminated against in many of those journals.

## Are Paid Reviews Worth It?

Before considering a paid review service, think carefully about your goals, who you are targeting, and whether the money could be better spent elsewhere. You may want to exhaust your sources for free reviews first before considering paid reviews.

Librarians and booksellers know which publications do paid reviews, so reviews from those sources are not likely to carry much weight with them. On the other hand, paid reviews may be seen by consumers and they could generate good quotes for book marketing purposes.

If you do use paid reviews, be cautious about spending too much—some of these services charge more than $400 for a review. How many extra books will the review have to sell to recoup that investment?

Some of the online review services will post the review on Amazon and a number of other online sites, which might be worth a modest fee. However, Amazon's policies do prohibit the posting of paid reviews, and they have been known to remove reviews from companies that offer this service.

## Review Sources

Listed below are several review sources. Inclusion on this list is not a recommendation, but rather a starting point for your research. Do your homework and only consider paid reviews in light of your overall book review strategy.

Two of the traditional book review journals have launched paid review publications in recent years:

- *Kirkus Indie* is from the publisher of *Kirkus Reviews*. Reviews are published on KirkusReviews.com and some reviews are selected to be featured in the mainstream *Kirkus Reviews* magazine or their email newsletter. Learn more at:
http://www.kirkusreviews.com/indie/about

- *Clarion* is produced by the publisher of *ForeWord Reviews*. Reviews are posted on the ForeWord website and licensed to the three top wholesale databases. See details at: http://bit.ly/ohhHtf or

    http://www.forewordreviews.com/
    services/bookreviews/clarion-review/

Below are links to several other reviewers that offer paid reviews:

**Blue Ink Reviews** was founded by literary agent Patricia Moosbrugger, and former book review editor of the *Rocky Mountain News*, Patti Thorn. This service focuses on self-published books and they do accept ebooks.

Learn more at: http://www.blueinkreview.com

**Review The Book** (owned by Reader Views) charges a $25 administrative fee to list your book for their team of reviewers to request review copies. Up to five reviewers can request a book and each reviewer who accepts a book is obligated to post their review on ten different websites. You aren't guaranteed a review if none of their reviewers selects your book. The reviewers are compensated only with a free book; they are not paid.

Go to http://reviewthebook.com/index.php/home/faq/24 for details on Review the Book and visit http://www.readerviews.com for information on their regular Reader Views review service

**Reader Spoils** charges $97 for a listing in a twice-monthly newsletter distributed to more than 8,900 people who signed up to review books. Authors designate how many review copies they want to distribute and they are expected to provide a token payment or gift (such as $10 cash or $5 Starbucks gift card) to each person who posts a review. Learn more at http://readerspoils.com/authors.html.

**Book Rooster** charges an administrative fee of $67 per book to invite suitable reviewers to review the book, to distribute the book (in mobi/Kindle format) to people who have agreed to review it, and to make sure at least ten reviews have been submitted to Amazon by their reviewers.

http://www.bookrooster.com/for-authors/

**Heartland Reviews** was founded by independent bookstore owner Bob Spears. See details at http://bit.ly/pWYIL1 or

http://www.heartlandreviews.com/Publisher_Submissions_and_Benefi.html.

## 10

# Book Review Journals

Book review journals are designed primarily for the book trade (libraries and booksellers) to help them make book buying decisions. The reviews are usually brief, due to space limitations and the need for their readers to peruse the listings quickly.

Some publications review only certain types of books and some only review prior to or within a certain time after publication. Other journals do post-publication reviews, usually within three months of publication.

## The Importance of Reviews to Libraries and Bookstores

Because budgets are tight and staff are very busy, librarians consider reviews in trade journals to be their most important and trusted source of information about books. There's simply no way for librarians to keep up with the hundreds of thousands of books being published each year, and they value the screening process and objectivity of the journals.

A good review in a major journal can result in many library sales. In fact, some libraries automatically purchase some or all of the books that are reviewed in their favorite journals.

To learn more about how to sell your books to libraries, see *The Savvy Book Marketer's Guide to Selling Your Book to Libraries* at www.SellingtoLibraries.com.

Bookstore buyers also find the review journals, particularly *Publishers Weekly*, to be vital sources of information about new books.

If you have a publisher, make sure they are sending review copies out to the appropriate journals in a timely manner. If you're the publisher, make this a priority. Unfortunately, the journals can review only a small percentage of the huge number of books submitted to them.

## Savvy Tip

Research the websites and editorial calendars of the journals for other opportunities to get mentioned. For example, some journals have columns where they list award-winning books, or they do roundup articles mentioning several books on a particular topic.

Below are links to the submission guidelines for some of the most important book review journals. Eligibility and submission instructions vary by publication, so be sure to **read the requirements carefully and submit EXACTLY what is required**.

## Pre-Publication Reviewers

Pre-publication reviews are solicited before the official publication date (or on sale date) of the book. These journals need to receive books at least three months prior to publication so that they have time to assign the book to a reviewer, get the review written, and publish the review near the book's publication date. However, some of the journals have relaxed their requirements somewhat, so read the rules carefully.

As explained in chapter 3, pre-publication reviewers expect to receive a galley (or advance reading copy) because the final book is not yet printed three months prior to publication. This is a bound copy of the almost finished book, which still may be in the final proofreading stages.

There is no point in sending an already published book and claiming a publication date three months in the future. It's easy for the reviewer to check the actual publication date on Amazon.com.

Here's a list of the major pre-publication reviewers:

- ***Publishers Weekly*** – for books available in bookstores only. See http://bit.ly/peQNbT or

  http://www.publishersweekly.com/pw/corp/submissionguidelines.html

- ***Library Journal*** – http://bit.ly/nl72TB or

  http://www.libraryjournal.com/csp/cms/sites/LJ/SubmitToLJ/TitlesForReview.csp

- ***Booklist*** – published by the American Library Association.

  http://www.booklistonline.com/GeneralInfo.aspx?id=65

- ***Kirkus Reviews*** – http://bit.ly/pC5Q69 or

http://www.kirkusreviews.com/kirkusreviews/about_us/submission.jsp

- *ForeWord Reviews* – focuses on independently published books. See http://bit.ly/pIbI7v or

  http://www.forewordreviews.com/get-reviewed/submission-guidelines/

- *Bulletin of the Center for Children's Books*
  http://bccb.lis.uiuc.edu/pubguide.html

- *Quill & Quire* is the magazine of the Canadian book trade and they review new adult and children's titles.

  http://www.quillandquire.com/about.cfm
  http://www.quillandquire.com/faq.cfm#29

## Post-Publication Reviewers

Send review copies to these journals immediately upon publication. They usually publish reviews within three months of publication.

- *Midwest Book Review* – friendly to small presses and indie publishers; caters to the book trade and to consumers.
  http://www.midwestbookreview.com/get_rev.htm

- *Choice* – for academic libraries.
  http://www.ala.org/acrl/choice/forthcoming or
  http://www.ala.org/acrl/choice/selectionpolicy

- *The Horn Book* – children's and young adult titles.
  http://www.hbook.com/about-us/submissions/

- *School Library Journal* – children's and young adult titles. http://bit.ly/qHkKJ5 or

    http://www.schoollibraryjournal.com/csp/cms/sites/SLJ/Info/submissions.csp

- *Science Books & Films* – science-based books, videos, and software for all ages. Submission information is near the bottom of this page:

    http://www.sbfonline.com/pages/faq.aspx

## Other Reviewers

Browse this list of lesser-known publications for review sources that are a good fit with your book's topic:

http://www.libdex.com/journals.html

## Case Study – Midwest Book Review

If your book is self-published or published by a small press, be sure to submit it to *Midwest Book Review*, which has long been a champion of small and independent publishers. Below is a description of the review services that they provide.

"The *Midwest Book Review*, despite its name, has a global reach with respect to where our reviews wind up. In addition to our nine monthly online book review magazines, we are also content providers for Amazon.com. We also have a contract with Cengage Learning - Gale (formerly known as Thomson-Gale) who provides our reviews to several other online databases including Lexus-Nexus (primarily for academicians and journalists), as well as Goliath and Book Review Index (designed for corporate, academic, community, and governmental librarians). Additionally, our reviews are posted to thematically appropriate online discussion groups. All-in-all, we have a circulation of 30,000+.

When we send publisher's a copy of a review of their book, we also include a 'publisher notification' letter that details which (and what issues) of our publications the review appears in. For example, reviews originally published in *The Bookwatch*, *The Library Bookwatch*, and *The Wisconsin Bookwatch* are also automatically published in *The Internet Bookwatch*.

Our reviews for preschool through young adult children's books are also utilized by the Children's Books Reference Department at the Helen C. White Library on the University of Wisconsin, Madison, campus. This is a service utilized by school and community children's librarians throughout the state.

We also archive the reviews on our own *Midwest Book Review* website for five years. Our *Children's Bookwatch* archives get about 400 to 500 hits every month."

Jim Cox, Editor-in-Chief, *Midwest Book Review*,
www.MidwestBookReview.com

## Working with Review Journals

It's important to understand that book review journals can only accept a small percentage of the books submitted for review—maybe 10 to 15 percent of submissions get reviewed. (One exception is *Midwest Book Review*, where the percentage of books reviewed is close to 30 percent.) This means that many excellent books are rejected for lack of space, rather than lack of quality.

It also means that books that are not produced to industry standards (well written and edited, and well laid out with a professional looking cover) stand virtually no chance of getting reviewed. With so many quality books to choose from, the review journals must narrow down the piles of incoming books based on certain criteria.

Many of the larger journals have a bias against independently published books, especially those printed by the print-on-demand method. There is still a misconception in the book trade about subsidy publishing vs. print-on-demand as a method of printing books, and many equate POD with low quality. If your POD book was professionally produced and is available through Ingram or Baker & Taylor, consider submitting it to the journals that specify "no print-on-demand books."

## 11

# Print Media

The previous chapter covered book review journals that are geared primarily to librarians and booksellers. In this chapter we will look at publications that are designed for consumers, including newspapers, literary magazines, general magazines, and trade magazines.

## Mass Market Newspapers

Newspapers (and their staffs) are shrinking due to competition from online media and lower ad revenue. Many newspapers have dropped their book review sections, and the ones that remain usually review books from major publishers.

*The New York Times Book Review*, the most well-known newspaper reviewer, does pre-publication reviews for books available in bookstores only. Details are at http://www.nytimes.com/content/help/site/books/books.html#booksq02

*USA Today* publishes best seller lists, but they only review a handful of books a week and these are most likely from major publishers.

Some local newspapers review books from local authors or books of local interest—find a way to make your book relevant. Your local newspaper or business journal may also cover your book launch party or other events that you are doing.

In general, it's easier to get coverage in newspapers outside of the book review page. Try pitching a feature story or news story about you, the subject matter of your book, or something unusual that you are doing.

Recently a publisher in Sweden got some great press coverage after staging a book signing onboard a commercial flight. You don't need to do something quite that dramatic to get coverage, but you do need to stand out. Think about what kind of story angle would make for interesting reading for the public. What makes your book unique? How does it make the world a better place? What makes you different from thousands of other authors? Why should the reporter or their readers care about you, your book, or the topic that you write about?

## Case Study – Newspaper Book Reviews

Terry Whalin, author of *Jumpstart Your Publishing Dreams: Insider Secrets to Skyrocket Your Success* and other books, shares this story:

Janice Harayda, who worked for 11 years as the book review editor for the *Plain Dealer* in Cleveland, wrote a column for *Publishers Weekly* titled Critics Don't Need Free Books. She said, "At the *Plain Dealer*, I got more than 400 books a week from publishers, a landslide hard to handle even with another person helping me."

See the long odds to get your book reviewed in a major city newspaper? It's somewhere in the range of four books get reviewed out of over 400 books that are received. So do you give up and not try to get book reviews? No, you simply try more niche oriented markets where the probability is more likely of getting your book reviewed."

## Literary Magazines and Newspapers

Literary publications discuss books and authors and are geared to consumers, although some are more academic in nature. Listed below are some examples:

*Book Page* is a tabloid-size book review paper that's distributed free in libraries. They require galleys three months in advance and say, "We do not give review consideration to self-published books, print-on-demand titles or books from presses that lack major distribution."

See http://bookpage.com/content/submission-guidelines

*The Bloomsbury Review* is a book review magazine published quarterly and distributed by subscription and through bookstores, libraries, and newsstands in the United States and Canada. It includes book reviews, interviews with writers, profiles, essays, and poetry. The editors look for "well-written, interesting books by new and emerging writers that are unlikely to get a review in the larger publications." They do accept books from small presses and independent publishers and they review newly released books or bound galleys.

See http://www.bloomsburyreview.com/getreviewed.html

**1776 Productions** produces free local book review newspapers in San Francisco and Sacramento, and licenses a book review publication in Portland (and soon in Denver). They also publish reviews on their websites. Reviews are given to books published within the past 6 months, and self-published books are accepted. Reviews of books written by local authors will be identified within the publications and on the websites. Their pool of more than 120 reviewers choose which books to review from books submitted by publishers and self-published authors.

*San Francisco Book Review* and *Sacramento Book Review* are both owned by 1776 Productions. Authors/publicists submitting books for consideration should send books to the Sacramento address. Because *Portland Book Review* is licensed from 1776 Productions, books for that publication should be mailed to the Portland address.

1776 Productions also offers guaranteed reviews for a fee. See these links for submission guidelines:

- **San Francisco Book Review**
  http://sanfranciscobookreview.com/book-submission/
- **Sacramento Book Review**
  http://www.sacramentobookreview.com
- **Portland Book Review**
  http://www.portlandbookreview.com/submission-guidelines-2/

**New Pages** reviews books from independent publishers and small presses. http://www.newpages.com/faq.htm

**Romantic Times** covers the romance genre. Because they request galleys or ARCs, they probably want to receive them three months in advance. See

http://www.rtbookreviews.com/magazine/editorial-submissions

**Locus Magazine** features book reviews and news for science fiction and fantasy books. See the submission guidelines at http://www.locusmag.com/Home/FAQ.html#review.

See these pages for more links to literary and book review publications:

- Literary Magazines
  http://www.newpages.com/literary-magazines/

- Book Review Magazines
  http://www.bookmarket.com/magazines-books.htm

- Fiction, Poetry and Literary Journals
  http://www.bookmarket.com/magazines-fiction.htm

## Magazines and Newsletters

Like newspapers, many magazines are struggling with falling ad revenue and online competition, and their page counts are shrinking. The consumer magazine business includes general interest magazines as well as specialty magazines geared to niche topics such as knitting, horse training, or sailing.

Many magazines do brief book reviews or mention books in articles related to the book's topic. Magazines tend to be biased toward larger publishers, but may be open to other books that are a very close fit for their audience. The writers of magazine articles often quote authors of books who are experts on a topic they are writing an article about, and some magazines accept feature articles written by authors.

Check the magazine's editorial calendar to see if there are any special issues or features coming up that are a good fit for your book. It's also a good idea to subscribe to a media alert service such as HARO at http://www.helpareporter.com, where freelance writers post requests for experts on particular topics.

Trade magazines and newsletters are a potential source of reviews for nonfiction books. Trade magazines are designed for people who work in a particular industry or profession. Many of them are published by trade associations and professional societies.

Don't overlook newsletters that are published by hobby clubs related to your book's topic. To make it economically feasible to send review copies, try to seek out those with a fairly large membership as well as those in your local area where you can make personal contacts.

## Researching Media Contacts

It's important to contact the right media outlet and the right person. You may need to use a combination of sources to find the information you need.

Public libraries usually subscribe to directories of media and associations, and many of these are now available online to library cardholders. Check your library website or call the reference desk to inquire.

If you know the specific publication you are looking for, do an online search for their website. This is a great way to get the most current information, including editor names, editorial calendars, and even email addresses. But the website might not contain as much detail as a media directory.

There are also several online media directories. For example, you can buy a one-day subscription to search the magazine database at Wooden Horse Publishing at http://www.woodenhorsepub.com/.

John Kremer, author of *1001 Ways to Market Your Books*, maintains several media lists on his website, including these:

- Newspapers
  http://www.bookmarket.com/newspapers.htm

- Top General Magazines
  http://www.bookmarket.com/magazines.htm (look in the left column for links to magazines by category)

## Tips for Working with the Media

When dealing with the media (other than book reviewers) it's a good idea to query first, rather than sending a book. If you see that a writer or columnist has already reviewed or mentioned a book somewhat similar to yours, mention that in your query. Keep your communication brief and make it as easy as possible for the person to help you. See chapter 3 for more tips on sending queries.

Techniques for working with the media to get press coverage are outside the scope of this book, but a number of literary publicists and other experts have offered media tips on The Savvy Book Marketer blog. Here are links to several articles:

- Free Report – How to Book Radio Shows and Be a Great Guest, by Larry James
  http://bit.ly/id8HKF

- Anatomy of a Successful Press Release for Book Promotion, by Carol White
  http://bit.ly/q1i254

- Tips for Writing Effective News Releases for Your Self-Published Book, by Sue Collier
  http://bit.ly/gkBeLP

- How to Develop Key Messages and Get Them Across Quickly, by Jackie O'Neal
  http://bit.ly/atLYTt

- Book Publicity Tips for Fiction Authors, by Tolly Moseley
  http://bit.ly/djHOkp

- Building Author Platform by Pitching Yourself to the Media, by Nina Amir
  http://bit.ly/9Q0cg2

- Use the Calendar to Promote Yourself and Your Book, by Robin Hoffman
  http://bit.ly/dhSDWZ

- Fool-proof Ways to Correspond With Journalists, by Jackie O'Neal
  http://bit.ly/a8jZY9

Learn more about working with the media on The Savvy Book Marketer's Publicity Resources page at http://bit.ly/eMwtOB or http://bookmarketingmaven.typepad.com/resources/book-publicity-tips-for-authors.html.

## 12
## Other Book Review Sources

In this chapter you will find some additional ideas for getting book reviews that don't fit neatly into the standard review categories covered in other chapters. Use these as an inspiration to come up with your own creative ideas.

### Create Audio and Video Reviews

Invite customers and colleagues to do audio or video reviews of your book and post them on your website. There are several online services that make it easy for customers to record testimonial audios or videos.

For example, **AudioAcrobat** provides phone lines for customers to record testimonials about your books. Customers dial a number with a unique extension number to record their comments, and you can have different testimonial lines for each of your books. AudioAcrobat is also a great tool for creating a podcast. The service is about $20 a month but there's a 30-day free trial. Learn more at http://www.audioacrobat.com.

## Offer Review Copies in Publishing Poynters Marketplace

To request reviews on Amazon.com and other websites, you can place a free listing in Dan Poynter's ***Publishing Poynters Marketplace***, an email newsletter with a circulation of more than 41,000 authors and publishing folks.

See a sample issue of the newsletter at: http://bit.ly/yBFcSg

Subscribe to the newsletter at: http://bit.ly/y2hCGQ

Here are the submission instructions from Dan Poynter:

*If you want your book reviewed on Amazon.com, B&N.com, etc., list it here in Publishing Poynters Marketplace (no charge). You must be willing to send a book and promotional materials (review-book package) to readers of Publishing Poynters Marketplace who contact you (usually 5 to 10 copies). Include the number of pages in your description and for children's books, list the age level for which the book is written. Make sure the book is already listed at Amazon.com*

*Just send your request and description to DanPoynter@ParaPublishing.com*
*Draft your request so that I do not have to edit it. Make it SHORT (100 words max), no italics or bold type. Just describe the book in a few words; don't send a lengthy review of it. Lengthy submissions will be returned for rewriting or ruthlessly cut. Reviewers only need enough information to see if they have expertise and an interest in your category. Supply full contact information including your email address. Write the draft as it should appear so that I do not have to do more than Copy/Paste. Put "Review Wanted" in the subject line.*

## Get Reviews on EzineArticles.com

EzineArticles.com is the most popular article directory website, but many people don't realize that they allow book reviews to be posted on the site. See the book review page for examples: http://ezinearticles.com/?cat=Book-Reviews

Book reviews posted on this site must adhere to the same quality standards as their other articles. See the guidelines here: http://ezinearticles.com/editorial-guidelines.html

If you know people who write for EzineArticles.com you can ask them to write a review of your book and post it there. Another option is to sign up for a review service that posts on EzineArticles, such as **Reader Spoils** at: http://readerspoils.com/ezine-book-reviews.html

Here's a list of the book review categories to choose from: http://ezinearticles.com/category-guidelines.html

It's not practical for you to post other people's reviews of your book on EzineArticles. Their rules require that whatever you post be original material written by you.

It's hard to say how much visibility book reviews get on EzineArticles. It seems unlikely that readers will go to the site seeking book reviews, but people can find the reviews through search engines and bloggers who are looking for content could also reprint them on their own sites.

There are a number of other article directory sites where book reviews can be submitted. Some to consider are:

- ArticlesBase www.articlesbase.com
- Go Articles www.GoArticles.com
- Article Dashboard www.ArticleDashboard.com

- Isnare www.Isnare.com
- SelfGrowth.com www.selfgrowth.com

## Seek Bloggers to Review Your Book

In chapter 8 we discussed working with book bloggers, but book reviews can be found on many other types of blogs, including topical blogs and personal blogs.

Spend some time doing online research to identify the top blogs that relate to your book's subject matter or cater to the same target audience as your book. Once you locate potential blogs, be sure to search their blogroll or links area for links to other similar sites. Then offer review copies to your top prospects.

Most nonfiction authors can find numerous blogs that are geared toward their topic or target audience. For example, authors of children's books and parenting books will find plenty of parenting and educator blogs online.

Novelists may be able to get the attention of sites that are related to some aspect of the book. For example, if the main character in your book is a horse trainer, seek out blogs and websites that cater to horse trainers and horse enthusiasts.

Of course, reviews aren't the only the valuable content for bloggers. Authors can also offer to write guest posts for appropriate blogs.

## Case Study – Get Bloggers Buzzing About Your Book

Michael Stelzner, who is the founder and CEO of the website SocialMediaExaminer.com, notes that posting book reviews is a great way for topical bloggers to share hot tips and new ideas with their readers. He posted this notice on his blog to promote his new book:

### Want a chance to review a new book?

*On June 6, I'll be releasing my new book: Launch: How to Quickly Propel Your Business Beyond the Competition (Wiley). It will share the precise strategy and tactics we used to grow Social Media Examiner into a top blog.*

*I want to prove that a book can be popular without the traditional media or methods most authors use to promote their books.*

*I'm inviting up to 50 bloggers to review my new book on their blog and receive an extra copy they can give away to their readers.*

*Here's how you could win two free copies of my book:*

- *Apply here (it's quick and easy) by May 10.*
- *Agree to review the book between June 6 and June 30.*
- *Give away your second copy to your readers in a creative way.*

*I'll review the entries and select the bloggers who'll receive copies of the book.*

Michael used SurveyMonkey.com to collect the review requests, but you could also use an autoresponder service like Aweber or MailChimp. Be sure to check out the outstanding website that Michael created to promote his book:

http://socialmediaexaminer.com/launch

## A Little Help From Your Friends

In chapter 6 we talked about having friends and family post reviews on online bookstores. It can be tricky because you don't want reviews to sound like they were written by your mother or your best friend.

Another approach is to ask friends, family, business associates, and acquaintances to review or mention the book on their blog. If the review turns out to be helpful and objective, you can ask the person to post it on sites like Amazon or Goodreads too.

If you don't feel comfortable asking these folks to review your book, consider asking them to help spread the word through their personal blogs and social networks, or even email a few friends that they think would be a good fit for your book. They can post just a sentence or two announcing the book, without actually reviewing it.

## Check the Book Reviewers List at Writers in the Sky

Author and book editor Yvonne Perry of Writers in the Sky has put together a list of people who offer book review services. These folks do not necessarily maintain a book blog; they may just be posting on sites like Amazon or Goodreads. Be sure to read the list and the comments section at http://bit.ly/nXMsOb or

http://yvonneperry.blogspot.com/2009/01/book-reviewers-needed-for-list-of-book.html.

## Enter Book Award Programs

When you are a finalist or winner in a book award contest, you not only get to promote the award in your promotional materials, but you might also get a brief review or testimonial quote that you can use for book promotion. Not all award contests provide a brief critique/review, but some do.

*"Remember, an award can make the difference in getting a closer look by the media and getting you the coverage and ultimately the sales you seek."*

Kate Siegel Bandos<br>Literary publicist at KSB Promotions

There are numerous award programs to choose from, and the entry fees can really add up, so choose carefully. Below are links to several award programs. Make a note of the entry deadlines and fees for each program you're interested in and add it to your promotional calendar. Some award programs offer discounts for early entries. Be sure to read and follow the submission instructions carefully. Below are links to some of the largest competitions:

- Ben Franklin Awards, sponsored by IBPA, is the most prestigious award for independent publishers.
  http://www.pma-online.org/pubresources/benfrank.aspx

- Independent Publisher Book Awards (IPPY)
  http://www.independentpublisher.com/ipland/IPAwards.php

- Writer's Digest Self-Published Book Awards
  http://www.writersdigest.com/selfpublished

- National Indie Excellence Book Awards
  http://www.IndieExcellence.com

- Next Generation Indie Book Awards
  http://www.indiebookawards.com/index.php

There are also award competitions geared toward specific types of books. Here are a few:

- RITA Awards from Romance Writers of America
  http://www.rwa.org/cs/contests_and_awards

- Moonbeam Children's Book Awards
  http://www.moonbeamawards.com/

- Dan Poynter's Global eBook Awards
  http://GlobalEbookAwards.com

- Audies Audio Book Awards
  http://www.theaudies.com/

- Axiom Business Book Awards
  http://www.axiomawards.com/

- Living Now lifestyle book awards
  http://www.livingnowawards.com/

- Nautilus Book Awards
  http://www.nautilusbookawards.com/

For more ideas, see John Kremer's book awards list: http://www.bookmarket.com/awards.htm.

Here are some excellent articles about book awards from the After the Manuscript book marketing column on the San Francisco and Sacramento Book Review website:

- Are Book Awards Worth It?, by Kate Bandos, KSB Promotions
  http://bit.ly/pkHRuO

- Finding Appropriate Book Award Competitions to Enter, by Kate Bandos, KSB Promotions
  http://bit.ly/qK9EkY

- Leveraging Book Awards, by Stephanie Barko, Literary Publicist
  http://bit.ly/frDTPN

## 13

# Review Other Authors' Books

Most of this book focuses on getting people to review your book, but it can be beneficial to write reviews of other books that appeal to your same target audience.

You are doing the other authors a favor by reviewing their books, and it can be a good start to developing relationships. They might return the favor for you, or perhaps you can find other ways to work together.

You could even ask several other authors if they would like to exchange reviews with you, but be careful that you aren't crossing a line into questionable practices that could be seen as trying to take advantage of the review system. It's a good idea to only exchange reviews with books that you know to be of good quality.

The authors of books that you review are likely to share your review with their own followers, through posting on their social networks, blog and newsletter. But it never hurts to give them a gentle reminder. Providing a shortened link that they can post on social networks is a subtle but effective tactic.

Posting reviews on online bookstores like Amazon gives you visibility directly where people are shopping for books similar to yours. Online bookstore reviews are discussed in more detail below.

You can also post book reviews on reader networks like Goodreads and on your own blog. Reviewing complementary (but not directly competitive books) on your blog gives you the chance to provide useful content to your readers while doing the book's author a favor. You may be invited to participate in a virtual book tour by doing a book review.

A book review that has been keyword optimized may attract new visitors to your blog through online searches.

You can even earn money from your book reviews by signing up for the author's affiliate program (if they have one) or joining the Amazon Associates affiliate program. Don't expect to get rich from Amazon Associates, but every little bit helps.

**Savvy Tip**

Although I normally shop at Amazon, I ordered a book on BN.com several years ago so that I would be able to post reviews on the site. I recommend that you do the same if you don't already have an account at BN.com. In addition to being able to post reviews, signing into your account will give you access to some areas of the site that you could not otherwise access.

**How to Write Book Reviews**

It's important for reviews to sound authentic. One way to do that is to mention something specific that you liked about the book, rather than just praising it. For nonfiction, it's good to share a tip or idea from the book. Of course, you want to avoid spoilers (giving away the ending or too much of the story) in fiction reviews.

When you review a book on your blog, include the basic facts such as book title, author name, publisher name, and link to where the book can be purchased. Professional reviewers may also include the year of publication, page count and perhaps ISBN, but that's not really necessary on a blog with a hyperlink to the book's sales page.

On online bookstores you will need to give the review a title. Try to be creative and make it stand out, rather than saying something generic like "great book." Look at the titles of other reviews for the same or similar books to get a feel for good titles.

For extra exposure, post a video book review on Amazon (file size limit 100MB and maximum length 10 minutes).

When reviewing other books, it's important to avoid the appearance of being overtly promotional, and of course you don't want to disparage your competitors. It's possible to make subtle references such as these:

> *"As a thriller author myself, I really appreciated the twists and turns of the plot…"*
>
> *"As a book marketing coach, I know how important social marketing is, and this book does a terrific job of explaining how to gain a following on Facebook."*

Mentioning the type of books that you write actually makes you look like an authority on the subject and gives your review more credibility.

You can sign your name at the bottom of the review, along with your book title, like this:

— Dana Lynn Smith, author of *Facebook Guide for Authors*

However, some people think that listing your book title in your reviews is too promotional and there have been reports of some reviews being deleted when the author of the book complained. Do NOT link to your own book when posting a book review on Amazon. It's against their rules and it looks tacky.

Your Amazon user name and "signature" will appear at the top of the review, and users can click through to view your personal profile on Amazon (which should include the names of your books and a link to your website).

Before you start writing reviews, be sure to update your Amazon "signature" on your personal profile. You have about 25 characters to showcase your specialty, genre, or brand name. For example:

- Romantic suspense author
- Social marketing expert
- The Productivity Pro

My signature on Amazon is "The Savvy Book Marketer," so all reviews that I post on the site are listed as being from "Dana Lynn Smith, The Savvy Book Marketer." Here's a sample review—notice how my signature at the top gives credibility to the review.

> ★★★★★ **No more excuses for not blogging!**, June 7, 2011
> By **Dana Smith "The Savvy Book Marketer"** (Texas) - See all my reviews
> REAL NAME
>
> This review is from: **No More Blank Screen: Blogging Ideas for Fiction Authors (Kindle Edition)**
> Many novelists fail to take full advantage of blogging as a promotional tool because they just aren't sure what to write about. With "No More Blank Screen: Blogging Ideas for Fiction Authors," there's no more excuse for not blogging! This book is packed with practical advice to help novelists promote their books through blogging. Highly recommended."

Learn more about writing reviews in the article, "How to Write a Book Review," by Rachelle Money at http://bit.ly/q6yLP9, and also see the article below, courtesy of Nick Daws.

## Case Studies – 7 Ways to Write Great Book Reviews

*Article by Nick Daws, reprinted with permission.*

Book reviewing is an art, and some people are better at it than others. If you're not too confident about reviewing, here are my top tips to set you on the right path...

When reviewing novels and other fiction, always follow the golden rule – never give away the whole plot!

In fact, there is little point simply in describing what happens in a novel anyway, since this will certainly be covered in the blurb. Instead, talk about things you liked and disliked, what you thought of the characters, what aspects of the novel you found particularly moving or memorable, and so on.

Study other people's reviews, especially the top reviewers on Amazon. See what makes their reviews so popular and effective, and try to incorporate what you learn in your own reviewing.

At the same time, though, try to develop your own style. Don't be afraid to include a few personal tidbits, e.g. by mentioning if your partner, child or dog enjoyed the book too! People love quirky, entertaining reviews, as long as they still impart useful information about the book.

With non-fiction books, think about who will be reading the book and why. This is especially important when reviewing "how-to" type books. Put yourself in the position of someone who wants to know whatever is set out in the book's title and description. In your review, discuss the extent to which you think the book lives up to its promises.

Try to avoid being entirely positive or entirely negative in your review. In the former case, readers are likely to conclude that you're a friend of the author or just trying to generate affiliate sales. In the latter case, they may conclude that you hold a grudge against them! Aim to provide a balanced review, saying honestly what you liked and what you didn't.

Finally, if you are reviewing a book on your own blog or website, don't forget to invite comments from your readers as well. Reader comments will generate more interest in the review itself, and will also help attract more search engine traffic in future.

So there you are - seven tips for writing book reviews. Happy book reviewing!

*Nick Daws is a UK-based freelance writer, editor and writing teacher at www.nickdaws.co.uk and he's also an Amazon Vine book reviewer.*

*For examples of how to write great book reviews, see Nick's reviews of Facebook Guide for Authors at http://bit.ly/iLQfO3 and Twitter Guide for Authors at http://bit.ly/ocrxmE.*

## Starting Your Own Review Site

Novelists who are avid readers may even want to set up a book review website and review books on a regular basis. As a promotional tool, this is most effective if you review books in your own genre. The authors of books that you review are likely to link back to your review site. You can promote your own books in the sidebar of your site below your photo and bio.

If you don't want to set up a separate review site, you could review other books occasionally on your blog – just be careful that it doesn't distract website visitors from focusing on your own books. Or you can put your reviews on a separate site and link to them from your main blog or website.

Keep in mind that managing a review site is a big investment of time and there will be expenses as well. Expenses can include postage costs if you are mailing books to a team of reviewers, travel to conferences, domains and web hosting fees, and design and technical assistance.

If you are thinking about setting up a review site or reviewing books on a regular basis, first read *The Slippery Art of Book Reviewing*, by Mayra Calvani and Anne K. Edwards, available at http://amzn.to/pDhGJ2. I read the Kindle version, but I recommend the paperback because you are going to want to do a lot of highlighting!

Even if you aren't planning to write many book reviews, this book will help you look at book reviews from the reviewer's perspective.

## 14

# How to Use Reviews to Promote Book Sales

This chapter explores how to use book reviews, endorsements and testimonials for maximum effectiveness in selling books, and includes examples from several authors.

## Where to Post Book Reviews

Where should you post your reviews, endorsements, and testimonials? Everywhere you can think of! Here are some suggestions:

- Selected pre-publication endorsements are usually printed on the back cover of books, and sometimes a blockbuster endorsement is placed at the top or bottom of the front cover. There's not much space on the cover, so you can also use endorsements on the first page or two inside the book.

- When you create free sample chapters for potential customers to download, be sure to include a list of endorsements and testimonial quotes at the beginning, and perhaps also at the end of the chapter. These provide "social proof" and put the reader in the frame of mind that what they are reading is valuable.

- Use endorsements, testimonial quotes and excerpts from reviews on all of your promotional materials, including the book's sales page on your website, your media room, bookmarks, brochures, etc.

- Consider creating a separate page on your website just for endorsements, testimonial quotes and excerpts from reviews, or place them in the sidebar of the website. You can also provide links to places where people can read the entire contents of reviews that have been excerpted, but it's generally not a good idea to use outbound links on a sales page because you don't want to distract them from clicking the buy button.

- Each time you get a new endorsement or book review, mention it on social sites like Twitter and Facebook and provide a link if possible. You can also write an occasional post on your blog or newsletter about your endorsement and reviews, publicly thanking the writers of them.

- Book reviews can be published on **Self-Publishing Review**. Be sure to get the permission of the reviewer or ask them to post the review for you. See submission requirements at
http://www.selfpublishingreview.com/submissions/.

- Novelist and book marketing expert Carolyn Howard-Johnson maintains the **New Book Review** website for authors and publishers to share their best reviews. The site was selected for the *Writers' Digest* "101 Best Websites for Writers" list. Be sure to read the submission guidelines in the left column at
http://www.thenewbookreview.blogspot.com.

- Use endorsements and testimonial quotes on your sell sheet, as discussed in chapter 3. You can use just a few quotes, or devote the entire back of the page to quotes.

## Tips for Using Reviews

Keep good records of all of the endorsements, testimonials and reviews that you have solicited and received, and keep copies of printed reviews and email correspondence in a convenient place where you can access them easily.

You should consult a writer's legal guide or intellectual property attorney for guidance on copyright issues related to the use of reviews, but this chapter offers some suggestions on how to use reviews.

It's generally understood that reviews in book review publications and book review blogs may be used by the author or publisher for promotional purposes, but be sure to ask if you have any doubts and give credit to the publication or site that published the review.

For endorsements and customer testimonials/reviews, get written permission to use the quote for promotional purposes.

Endorsements and testimonial quotes used for promotional purposes need to be short—usually just one or two sentences. It's usually acceptable to excerpt from a review or longer quote, so long as you don't distort the intention of the writer. If you would like to make a minor change in a testimonial or endorsement, just ask for permission.

For reviews that are printed in publications or on book blogs, it's customary to list the name of the publication or blog at the end of the review or review excerpt.

With endorsements and testimonials given by individuals, it's essential to sign the quote with a full name, not initials or something else that looks fake.

It's important to list credentials after the person's name, to establish the credibility of the person being quoted and to avoid the appearance of "made up" quotes. For example, an endorsement for your book on horse training might be signed with "John Jones, winner of three national show jumping championships." A company name may also be used if it's relevant.

When quoting people who don't have professional qualifications related to a nonfiction book, it's best to find some kind of tagline to add to their name that demonstrates why readers should pay attention to what they say. Sometimes the person's age or location (city or state) are also used.

Using photos of the endorser or customer is a powerful way to make the quotes more believable and personal. Audio and video reviews can also lend credibility by showing that there's a real person behind the review, and they are also eye catching on a website.

When displaying a group of quotes or review excerpts, it's a good idea to arrange your quotes with the most impressive ones first.

## Using Reviews on Online Bookstores

Whenever customers give you good feedback on your book, remember to ask if they would be willing to post their comments on Amazon or BN.com.

Amazon claims copyright on all reviews posted on their site, so it's not a good idea to copy and paste their reviews to your website or other places. Other bookstores probably have similar policies. It would be safer to excerpt just one sentence, which could be considered fair use under copyright laws.

Amazon should automatically post reviews from the major review journals such as *Publishers Weekly* onto your book sales page on Amazon.com, although they don't state specifically which journals they work with. Here's an excerpt from their policies: "We license some reviews from other sources for some of the books we carry. For content we're licensed to reproduce, the original review will appear in its entirety."

If there are other reviews that you would like to showcase on your book sales page on Amazon, you can add brief excerpts to your book description.

> *"Amazon will publish 20-word review summaries on your book's detail page, relying on the fair use provision of copyright law."*
>
> Steve Weber
> author of *Plug Your Book! Online Book Marketing for Authors*

## Case Studies – How Authors Showcase Reviews

"I have found that using endorsements and testimonials really helps customers feel more confident in making the buying decision. When you have a big name endorser, it helps to stand on a rooftop and let everyone know as soon as they get to your site or page. For the second edition of *The Idea of America: What It Was and How It Was Lost*, we used Ron Paul's endorsement at the top of the book sales page at http://bit.ly/mRGMzh,"says Doug Hill of Laissez Faire Books.

* * * * *

Steven Lewis, author of *Kindle Formatting* and several other books, uses a WordPress plug in at the bottom of his home page at http://taleist.com to produce a rotating testimonial quote such as this:

**What they say**

 This is a great guide for the author getting into Kindle publishing. Well done. I've picked up a few tricks myself from it. Thanks for sharing.
– Tony Eldridge, Marketing Tips for Authors

"People who read my blog over time get to know me and, my experience has been, to trust me. The testimonials scroller is, however, on my homepage where visitors might not know me. The testimonials offer social proof of my bona fides and expertise, which is critical when you're selling online. You need clues to give buyers confidence that you're 'real' and you'll be around if they have a problem or question with your product. A blog is a great way to do that and so are testimonials," explains Steven.

\* \* \* \* \*

Novelist and book marketing expert Tony Eldridge capitalizes on his endorsement from bestselling author Clive Cussler by including a quote from Cussler in this standard author bio, which appears on his website and on articles he writes:

*Tony Eldridge is the author of the action/adventure book, The Samson Effect that Clive Cussler calls a "first rate thriller brimming with intrigue and adventure" and the Twitter marketing book, Conducting Effective Twitter Contests which helps people find targeted Twitter followers. He also shares his book marketing tips with fellow authors through his blog and through his free video marketing tips for authors. You can follow him on Twitter @TonyEldridge.*

Promoting your book to the fans of the authors or experts who gave you endorsements is another great strategy.

"When I joined MySpace, I joined all the Clive Cussler fan groups and introduced myself and my book. In the first three months of my book sales, Cussler fans were responsible for over one third of my book sales," explains Tony. "It also led to an invitation to spotlight my book at the national Cussler Convention in Denver," he adds.

*****

Larry James, author of *How to Really Love the One You're With* and other books, has a page on his website at http://bit.ly/jfZUOE asking for reviews of his book. His testimonial quotes are listed at: http://www.celebratelove.com/endorsements.htm

Larry also performs wedding ceremonies and he encourages couples to give him a testimonial quote when he sends them a post-wedding email containing some tips for the bride about name changes.

"I have a special page on my wedding website called Rave Reviews that lists reviews I receive by e-mail and also has links to several other websites where brides and grooms can go to post their review," explains Larry.

"I also will occasionally post some quotes on my wedding blog under a title such as It's Really Terrific When Good People Say Nice Things About You," he adds. These same ideas can be applied to book testimonial quotes as well.

*****

Novelist Heather Wardell uses a free Javascript from http://www.phpjunkyard.com/random-text.php that randomly displays one of her review quotes on the bottom of her home page at http://www.heatherwardell.com

"I'm now on my sixth self-published novel, so I have a lot of reviews, but having just one on the front page seems a good way to let people see them without overwhelming them," says Heather, who is the author of *Life, Love, and a Polar Bear Tattoo* and other books.

## About the Author

Dana Lynn Smith helps authors and indie publishers learn how to sell more books through her how-to guides, blog, newsletter, and private coaching.

Dana has a degree in marketing and 27 years of marketing experience. Her 17 years of publishing experience includes 13 years overseeing book production, marketing, fulfillment, and bottom-line profitability at Hoover's Business Press.

Learn more on her media room at http://bit.ly/DanaLynn.

Connect with Dana through these networks:

- **Twitter:** http://twitter.com/BookMarketer
- **Facebook Page:** www.facebook.com/SavvyBookMarketer
- **Book Marketing Group:** http://bit.ly/SavvyMkt
- **Facebook Profile:** www.facebook.com/DanaLynnSmith
- **LinkedIn:** www.linkedin.com/in/DanaLynnSmith
- **Google Plus:** http://gplus.is/DanaLynnSmith
- **Goodreads:** http://www.goodreads.com/SavvyBookMarketing

# Resources for Authors and Publishers

### Savvy Book Marketer Blog
www.TheSavvyBookMarketer.com

Packed with practical tips for promoting nonfiction, fiction and children's books.

### Savvy Book Marketing Network
www.SavvyBookMarketingNetwork.com

Join this free network to get complimentary ebooks and reports, a newsletter filled with book marketing tips and resources, access to member-only events, and special discounts on Savvy Book Marketer products.

### Ebook Publishing & Marketing
www.SavvyEbookPublishing.com

Website devoted to ebook news and how-to information.

### Book Marketing Podcast
http://bit.ly/SavvyPodcast

Podcast devoted to book marketing tips and advice.

### Savvy Book Marketer Guides
www.SavvyBookMarketer.com

In-depth book marketing guides teach you the skills you need to sell more books.

- How to Sell More Books on Amazon
- Selling Your Book to Libraries
- Facebook Guide for Authors

- Twitter Guide for Authors
- Successful Social Marketing
- Virtual Book Tour Magic

# Free Report
## Book Review Resources

This free report, in PDF format, contains all of the website addresses listed in *How to Get Your Book Reviewed* and includes live hyperlinks to each site.

Get your free copy at
**http://bit.ly/ReviewBonusReport**

or

http://bookmarketingmaven.typepad.com/products/bonus-report-book-review-resources.html

www.ingramcontent.com/pod-product-compliance
Lightning Source LLC
Chambersburg PA
CBHW022006100426
42738CB00041B/623